# PLANET EARTH

## A 4.5-BILLION-YEAR STORY

Written by ANTHEA LACCHIA
Illustrated by SAM FALCONER

# PLANET EARTH

## A 4.5-BILLION-YEAR STORY

Written by ANTHEA LACCHIA
Illustrated by SAM FALCONER

**DK LONDON**
**Senior Editor** Michelle Crane
**Senior Art Editor** Rachael Grady
**Project Editor** Edward Pearce
**Managing Editor** Francesca Baines
**Managing Art Editor** Philip Letsu
**Production Editor** Dragana Puvacic
**Production Controller** Joss Moore
**Jacket Designers** Rachael Grady, Rashika Kachroo
**Jacket Editor** Edward Pearce

**Consultant** Derek Harvey

First published in Great Britain in 2026 by
Dorling Kindersley Limited
20 Vauxhall Bridge Road,
London SW1V 2SA

The authorised representative in the EEA is
Dorling Kindersley Verlag GmbH. Arnulfstr. 124,
80636 Munich, Germany

Copyright © 2026 Dorling Kindersley Limited
A Penguin Random House Company
10 9 8 7 6 5 4 3 2 1
001–344952–Apr/2026

All rights reserved.
No part of this publication may be used or reproduced in any manner for the purpose of training artificial intelligence technologies or systems. In accordance with Article 4(3) of the DSM Directive 2019/790, DK expressly reserves this work from the text and data mining exception.

A CIP catalogue record for this book
is available from the British Library.
ISBN: 978-0-2417-1687-8

Printed and bound in India

www.dk.com

Throughout this book you will find illustrations that show the sizes of animals compared with the height of a child or the size of their hand.

Represents an average 12-year-old girl
150 cm (4.9 ft) tall

Represents an average 12-year-old's hand
15 cm (6 in)

**MIX**
Paper | Supporting responsible forestry
FSC™ C018179

This book was made with Forest Stewardship Council™ certified paper – one small step in DK's commitment to a sustainable future.
Learn more at www.dk.com/uk/information/sustainability

# CONTENTS

| | |
|---|---|
| Deep time | 06–07 |
| The birth of Earth | 08–09 |
| Earth and Moon | 10–11 |

## EARLY EARTH

| | |
|---|---|
| Turbulent Earth | 14–15 |
| Earth's jigsaw | 16–17 |
| First life | 18–19 |
| Origins of life | 20–21 |
| Snowball Earth | 22–23 |
| The big thaw | 24–25 |

## AN EXPLOSION OF LIFE

| | |
|---|---|
| The first animals | 28–29 |
| Curious creatures | 30–31 |
| Life explodes | 32–33 |
| Power grab | 34–35 |
| Greening the land | 36–37 |
| Forests emerge | 38–39 |
| Fish out of water | 40–41 |

| | |
|---|---|
| How fossils form | 42–43 |
| Tropical oceans | 44–45 |
| Carbon swamps | 46–47 |
| The Great Dying | 48–49 |
| Mass extinctions | 50–51 |

# THE RISE OF DINOSAURS

| | |
|---|---|
| Jurassic seas | 54–55 |
| Ammonites | 56–57 |
| Taking flight | 58–59 |
| Evolution of birds | 60–61 |
| The arrival of flowers | 62–63 |
| Early pollinators | 64–65 |
| A dinosaur's world | 66–67 |
| Dinosaurs through time | 68–69 |
| Asteroid impact | 70–71 |
| Double disaster | 72–73 |

# THE AGE OF MAMMALS

| | |
|---|---|
| Continents collide | 76–77 |
| Making mountains | 78–79 |
| Tropical forests | 80–81 |
| Tropics transform | 82–83 |
| Freezing world | 84–85 |
| Super-sized penguins | 86–87 |
| A mammal's world | 88–89 |
| New connections | 90–91 |
| Mega flood | 92–93 |
| From desert to sea | 94–95 |
| Enter humans | 96–97 |
| Human migration | 98–99 |
| Life in the cold | 100–101 |
| Ice age giant | 102–103 |
| Future Earth | 104–105 |
| Back from the brink | 106–107 |
| Timeline of Earth | 108–109 |
| | |
| Glossary and index | 110–111 |
| Acknowledgments | 112 |

**The timescale of Earth's history is so vast, the following abbreviations have been used:**
BYA = billion years ago
MYA = million years ago
YA = years ago

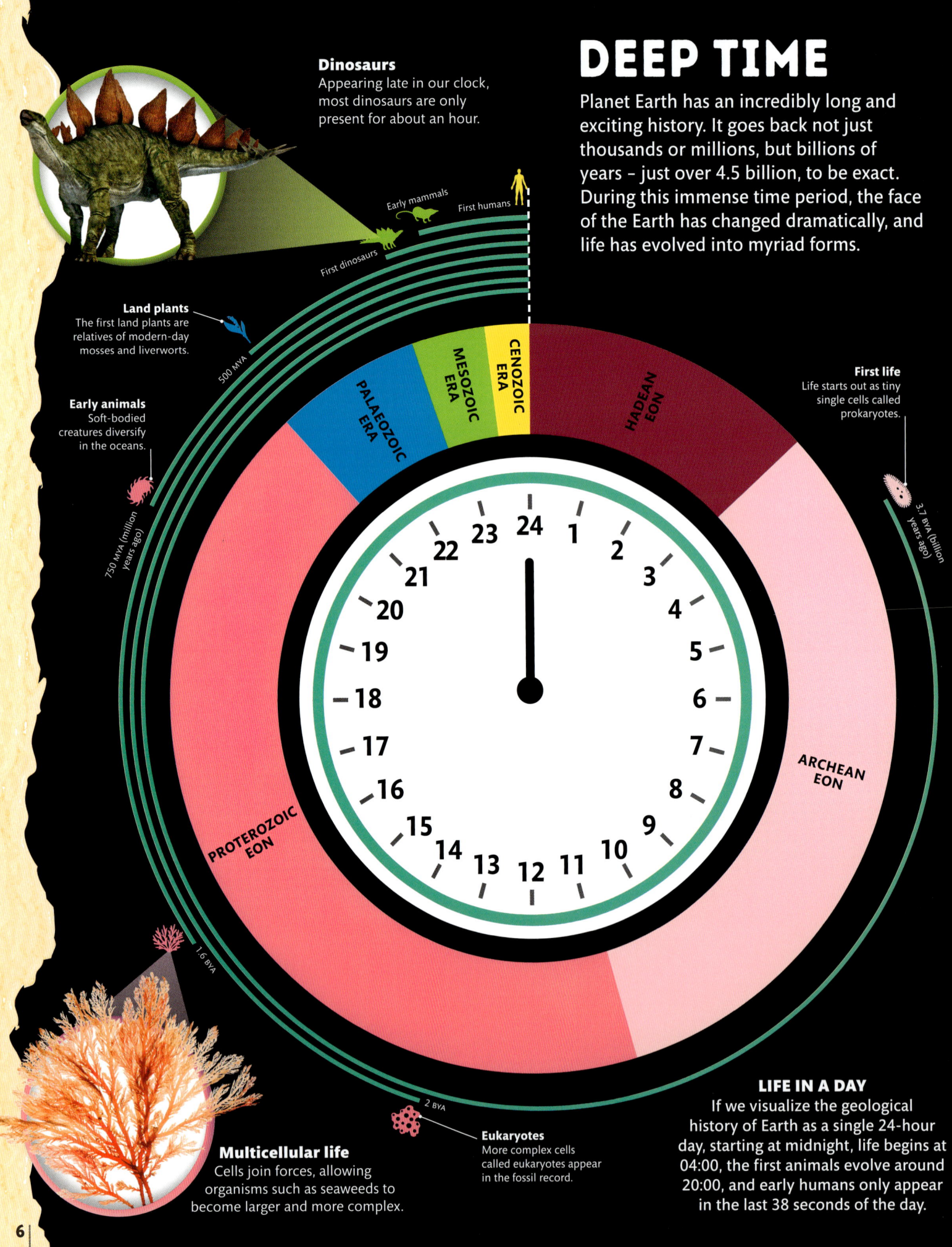

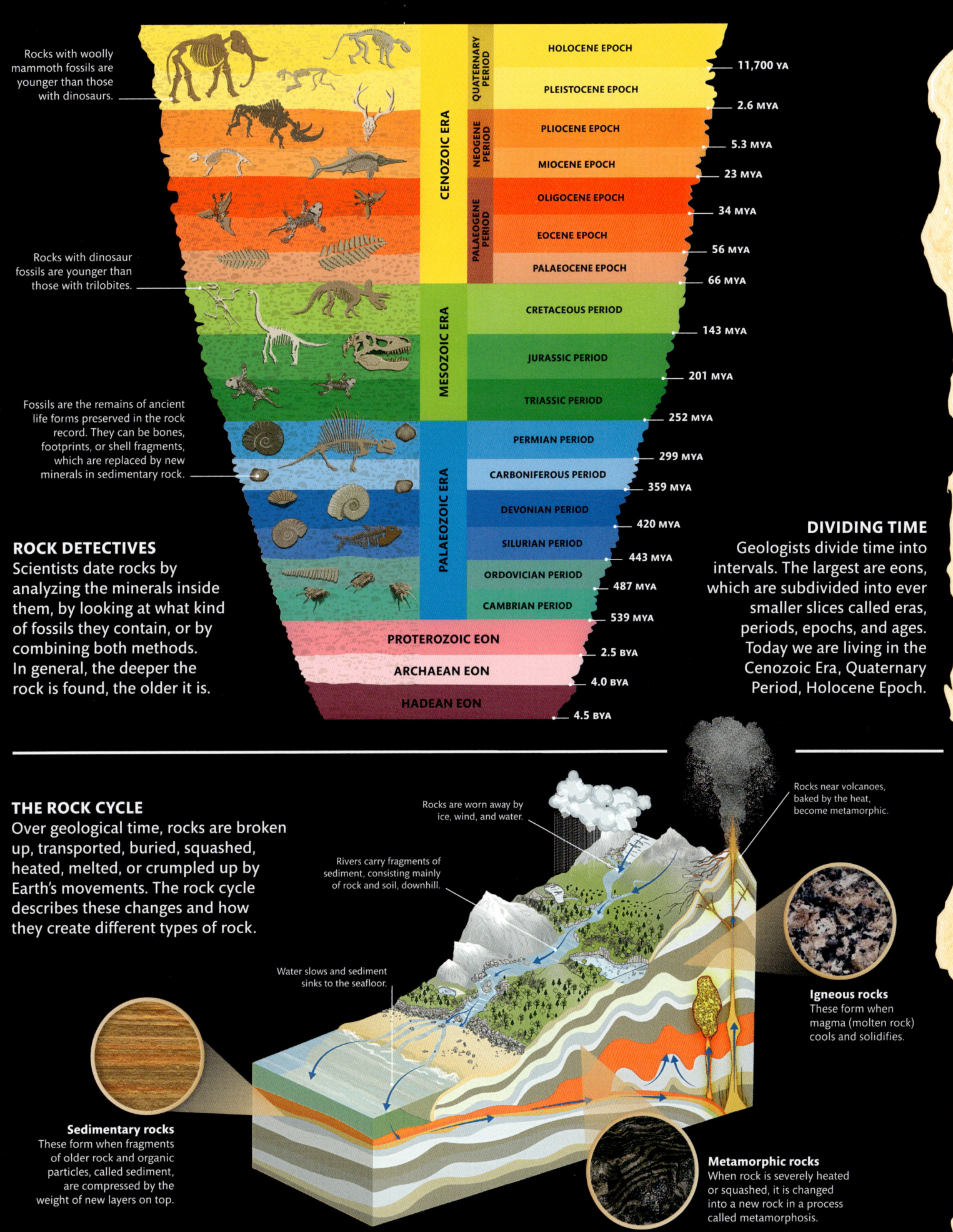

Rocks with woolly mammoth fossils are younger than those with dinosaurs.

Rocks with dinosaur fossils are younger than those with trilobites.

Fossils are the remains of ancient life forms preserved in the rock record. They can be bones, footprints, or shell fragments, which are replaced by new minerals in sedimentary rock.

## ROCK DETECTIVES
Scientists date rocks by analyzing the minerals inside them, by looking at what kind of fossils they contain, or by combining both methods. In general, the deeper the rock is found, the older it is.

## DIVIDING TIME
Geologists divide time into intervals. The largest are eons, which are subdivided into ever smaller slices called eras, periods, epochs, and ages. Today we are living in the Cenozoic Era, Quaternary Period, Holocene Epoch.

|  |  |  |  |
|---|---|---|---|
| CENOZOIC ERA | QUATERNARY PERIOD | HOLOCENE EPOCH | 11,700 YA |
| | | PLEISTOCENE EPOCH | 2.6 MYA |
| | NEOGENE PERIOD | PLIOCENE EPOCH | 5.3 MYA |
| | | MIOCENE EPOCH | 23 MYA |
| | PALAEOGENE PERIOD | OLIGOCENE EPOCH | 34 MYA |
| | | EOCENE EPOCH | 56 MYA |
| | | PALAEOCENE EPOCH | 66 MYA |
| MESOZOIC ERA | CRETACEOUS PERIOD | | 143 MYA |
| | JURASSIC PERIOD | | 201 MYA |
| | TRIASSIC PERIOD | | 252 MYA |
| PALAEOZOIC ERA | PERMIAN PERIOD | | 299 MYA |
| | CARBONIFEROUS PERIOD | | 359 MYA |
| | DEVONIAN PERIOD | | 420 MYA |
| | SILURIAN PERIOD | | 443 MYA |
| | ORDOVICIAN PERIOD | | 487 MYA |
| | CAMBRIAN PERIOD | | 539 MYA |
| PROTEROZOIC EON | | | 2.5 BYA |
| ARCHAEAN EON | | | 4.0 BYA |
| HADEAN EON | | | 4.5 BYA |

## THE ROCK CYCLE
Over geological time, rocks are broken up, transported, buried, squashed, heated, melted, or crumpled up by Earth's movements. The rock cycle describes these changes and how they create different types of rock.

Rocks are worn away by ice, wind, and water.

Rivers carry fragments of sediment, consisting mainly of rock and soil, downhill.

Water slows and sediment sinks to the seafloor.

Rocks near volcanoes, baked by the heat, become metamorphic.

**Igneous rocks**
These form when magma (molten rock) cools and solidifies.

**Sedimentary rocks**
These form when fragments of older rock and organic particles, called sediment, are compressed by the weight of new layers on top.

**Metamorphic rocks**
When rock is severely heated or squashed, it is changed into a new rock in a process called metamorphosis.

**1 Space rocks collide**
As collisions rattle the early Solar System, clumps of rock, dust, and metal stick together. One such clump is early Earth.

Only a tiny fraction of matter will form planets.

Planetesimals are tens to hundreds of kilometres in diameter.

**2 Young planet forms**
Early Earth, with a mass large enough for gravity's force to hold it together, becomes a sphere-shaped young planet, called a planetesimal.

As Earth grows, heavy particles gravitate towards the centre and lighter ones form layers around it.

**3 Earth grows up**
As it spins around the Sun, Earth pulls in more and more matter – from tiny dust grains to massive rocks – adding to its size.

# THE BIRTH OF EARTH

Most of Earth and everything that lives on it is formed from the remains of dead stars – even the elements that make up the human body are stardust. Earth's story begins 4.5 BYA when these starry remnants collapse into a spinning cloud of dust and gas around the young Sun.

**SPINNING DISC**
Planets such as Earth are born in clouds of gas and dust rotating around young stars such as our Sun. Gravity pulls matter towards the centre and the spin flattens it into a disc. Only a tiny fraction of the matter in the cloud forms planets – 99.9 per cent is pulled into the central Sun. The rest coalesces as clumps of rock, metal, ice, and gas.

**PLANET FORMATION**
Earth and the other planets within the Solar System form over tens of millions of years. Close to the Sun, rock and metal clumps merge into four rocky planets, including Earth. Further away, gas and ice condense into four gas giants.

**4.5 BYA: Hadean Eon**
As the clock started ticking, Earth's history began. Our infant planet was a ball of jumbled up space rocks, dust, and ice, held together by gravity. Violent impacts were constant, generating heat and melting Earth's surface.

Earth, like the other rocky planets Mercury, Venus, and Mars, develops layers – a crust, mantle, and core.

## SPACE ROCKS
Meteorites are extraterrestrial objects that fall to Earth's surface. Some contain elements of the first solid matter in the Solar System, so by dating them, we can estimate how old Earth is.

Collisions with space debris blast young Earth, heating and melting its rocks.

Vast oceans of lava cover the planet.

Earth's internal temperature probably reaches about 1,538°C (2,800°F).

**④ Fiery young planet**
Heat from impacts, and energy released from its core, causes Earth to melt. For hundreds of millions of years, it is a molten sea of magma.

## HOW THE MOON FORMED

The Apollo lunar missions of the 1960s and 1970s gathered rock samples from the Moon, providing important clues about its origin. The most likely theory is that it formed after a cosmic clash between Earth and another planet, Theia.

Theia struck Earth at a low angle, at an estimated speed of 14 km/s (8.7 mps).

Material from both planets was flung violently out into space.

**1 Giant impact**
About 60 million years after our planet first formed, a roughly Mars-sized body called Theia crashed into a young, still-molten Earth. The impact would have pulverized parts of both planets.

# EARTH AND MOON

From helping humans and birds find their way to stabilizing Earth's orbit and generating ocean tides, the Moon affects our planet in fascinating ways. But how it formed is a 4.5-billion-year mystery that scientists are still trying to unravel.

## TIDES

Ocean tides on Earth are caused by the Moon. As the Moon orbits around Earth, its gravity pulls a bulge of water to the near side of Earth, and throws another bulge outwards on the far side. As Earth spins on its axis, these two bulges remain in line with the Moon, giving most coastlines two high tides every day, with low tides in between.

The Moon's gravity pulls water to the near side of Earth.

Moon

Tidal bulges

Earth

Moon's orbit takes 27.3 days.

Earth's spin takes 24 hours.

On the far side of Earth, the Moon's gravity is weaker than at Earth's centre, but water is still pulled into a bulge.

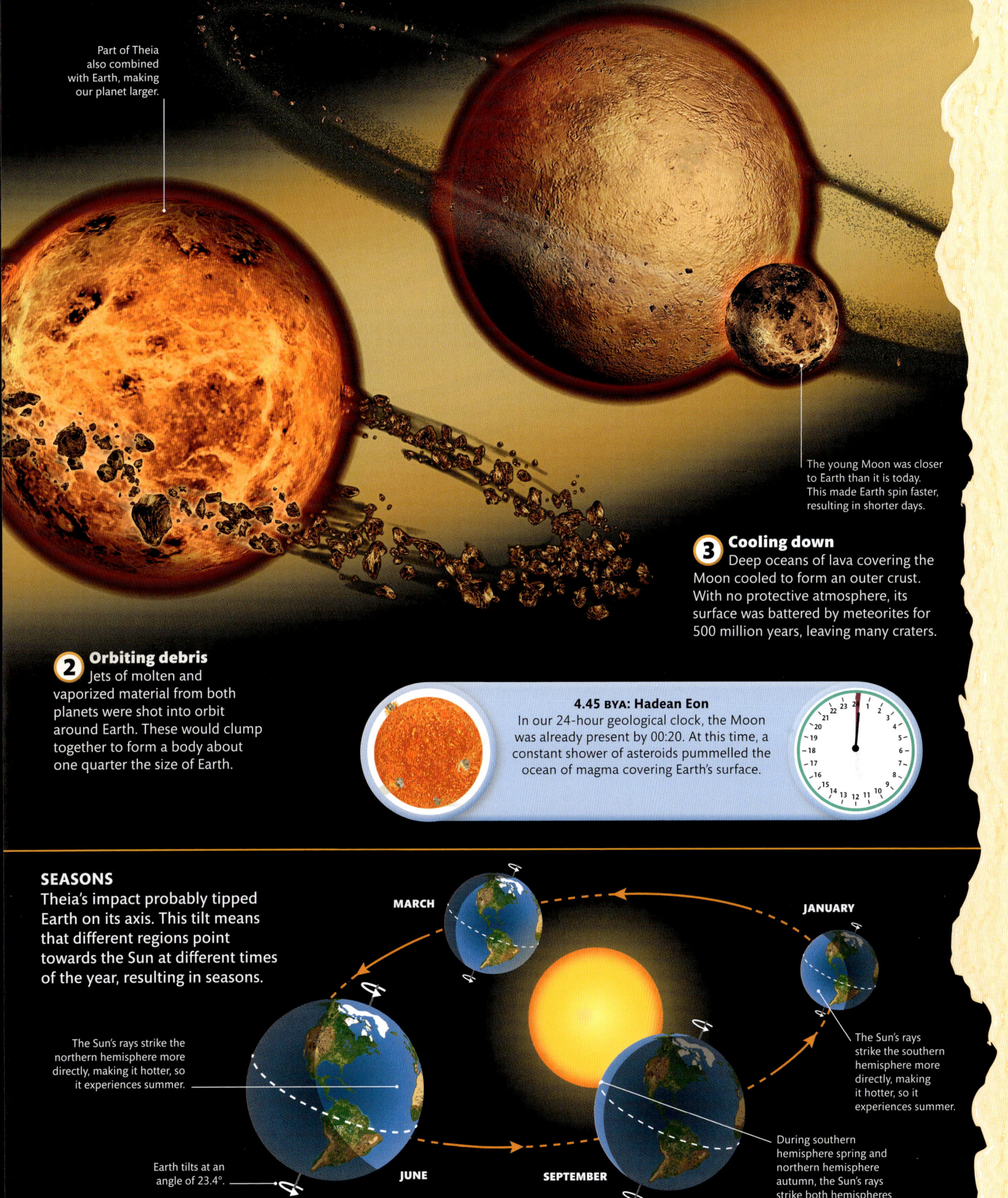

Part of Theia also combined with Earth, making our planet larger.

The young Moon was closer to Earth than it is today. This made Earth spin faster, resulting in shorter days.

**3 Cooling down**
Deep oceans of lava covering the Moon cooled to form an outer crust. With no protective atmosphere, its surface was battered by meteorites for 500 million years, leaving many craters.

**2 Orbiting debris**
Jets of molten and vaporized material from both planets were shot into orbit around Earth. These would clump together to form a body about one quarter the size of Earth.

**4.45 BYA: Hadean Eon**
In our 24-hour geological clock, the Moon was already present by 00:20. At this time, a constant shower of asteroids pummelled the ocean of magma covering Earth's surface.

## SEASONS
Theia's impact probably tipped Earth on its axis. This tilt means that different regions point towards the Sun at different times of the year, resulting in seasons.

The Sun's rays strike the northern hemisphere more directly, making it hotter, so it experiences summer.

Earth tilts at an angle of 23.4°.

MARCH

JANUARY

JUNE

SEPTEMBER

The Sun's rays strike the southern hemisphere more directly, making it hotter, so it experiences summer.

During southern hemisphere spring and northern hemisphere autumn, the Sun's rays strike both hemispheres at similar angles.

# EARLY EARTH

**Living fossil**
Stromatolites are rocky mounds of microbes – mostly known from 3.5-billion-year-old fossils. But these are rare living stromatolites, found in Australia's Shark Bay.

4.4–4.03 BYA HADEAN EON

# TURBULENT EARTH

The Hadean Eon is named after Hades, Greek god of the underworld. At this time, volcanoes spew lava onto a lifeless Earth. This solidifies into a primordial, stagnant crust. Earth is pummelled by meteorites made of debris floating around the early Solar System. Only tiny crystals of the mineral zircon survive from this time.

### 1 New Moon
A young Moon has formed and is visible from Earth. Our planet's only satellite is originally much closer to Earth, but has been moving away ever since at a rate of about 3.8 cm (1.5 in) per year.

### 2 Toxic atmosphere
Gases and steam released by volcanoes build up in a hot, toxic atmosphere that forms as Earth cools. Sunlight interacts with gases and particles to create a fiery orange glow. This early atmosphere contains hydrogen sulphide, methane, and 10 to 200 times as much carbon dioxide as today.

### 3 Pools of lava
Magma that reaches Earth's surface through erupting volcanoes gathers into incandescent pools, before solidifying into volcanic rocks. Water vapour released as the magma cools is thought to have contributed to the formation of the first oceans.

### 4 Space rocks
Early Earth is battered by incoming space debris in the shape of asteroids, meteors, and comets. These bombardments prevent the early crust from fully cooling and stabilizing. On the Moon, violent impacts form giant craters, which flood with magma.

### 5 Volcanic eruptions
Magma from Earth's mantle reaches the surface in violent volcanic eruptions. Under the sea, volcanoes spew out lava that solidifies to form volcanic islands. All this turbulent activity releases gases and water vapour into the atmosphere.

### 6 Crystallizing crust
Evidence from ancient grains of the mineral zircon found in Australia tells us that the first continents have formed at this time. These land masses are inactive, since tectonic plates have yet to begin moving.

# EARTH'S JIGSAW

During the Archaean Eon, Earth's surface became a much more dynamic place. Slowly, the hard crust that had developed in the Hadean Eon began to move, breaking into pieces called plates. It has been slowly moving ever since. This movement of plates is called plate tectonics.

## CONTINENTAL DRIFT

Have you ever noticed that Earth's continents fit together like puzzle pieces? This is because they were once joined together in supercontinents. Over time, several supercontinents have assembled and broken up again.

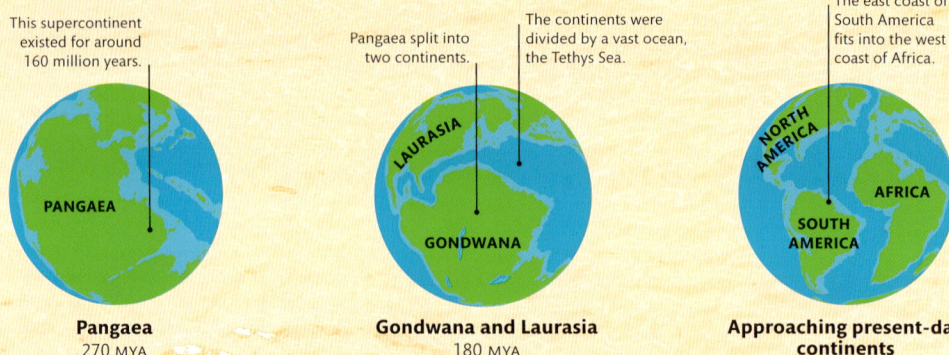

**Pangaea**
270 MYA
*This supercontinent existed for around 160 million years.*

**Gondwana and Laurasia**
180 MYA
*Pangaea split into two continents.*
*The continents were divided by a vast ocean, the Tethys Sea.*

**Approaching present-day continents**
66 MYA
*The east coast of South America fits into the west coast of Africa.*

## MOVING PLATES

Earth is divided into seven major tectonic plates. The plates are made of Earth's crust and the brittle top layer of the mantle. Their slow dance as they slide over the semi-molten lower layers of the mantle has created the continents and oceans as we know them today.

**Oceanic crust**
The crust under the oceans is thinner (7–10 km or 4–6 miles) and denser than the crust that forms continents.

**Mid-Atlantic Ridge**
New ocean crust is formed at mid-ocean ridges, where plates move apart, creating underwater mountains on the seafloor. This is an example of a divergent boundary.

**Mantle**
Semi-molten lower layers of the mantle below the crust allow plates to move.

## CRACKED CRUSTS

There are three types of boundaries between the plates: convergent, where two plates collide; divergent, where they spread apart from one another; or transform, where they slide past each other.

**North American plate**

**Eurasian plate**
This plate includes most of the Asian and European continents and oceanic crust under the Atlantic Ocean.

**Indo-Australian plate**

**Pacific plate**

**African plate**
The continental crust is 20–70 km (12.5–45 miles) thick and less dense than the oceanic crust, meaning it "floats" on the mantle above the oceans.

**South American plate**

**Antarctic plate**

## THE LAYERS OF EARTH

Earth can be thought of like an apple with three main layers: a hard skin on top, called the crust; a thick, softer middle, called the mantle; and a dense, metallic core in the very centre.

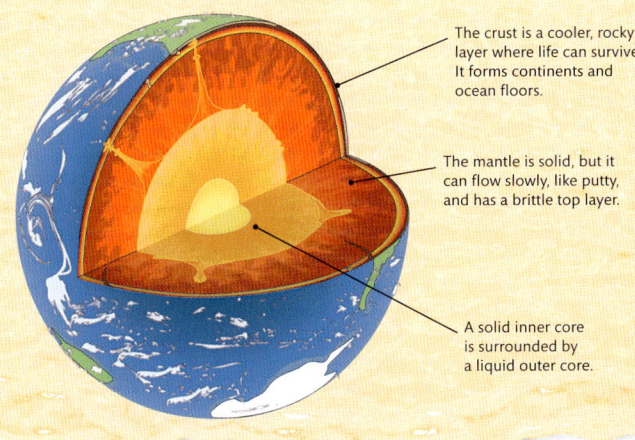

The crust is a cooler, rocky layer where life can survive. It forms continents and ocean floors.

The mantle is solid, but it can flow slowly, like putty, and has a brittle top layer.

A solid inner core is surrounded by a liquid outer core.

## MID-OCEAN RIDGE

In Iceland, it is possible to swim between two tectonic plates. This is a divergent boundary, where two plates are moving apart, and new crust is created at a rate of 2.5 cm (1 in) per year.

The boundary is part of the Mid-Atlantic Ridge, which extends 16,000 km (10,000 miles), mainly under the Atlantic Ocean.

## DRAGGED DOWN

When two plates collide, the denser plate will get dragged down under the other one. It will then be recycled in Earth's interior, in a process called subduction.

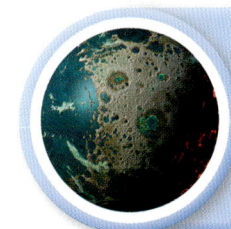 **4.1–3.2 BYA: Hadean to Archaean Eons**
The oldest known rocks formed about 02:00. When the asteroid bombardment of early Earth slowed down, the first continents were able to form. Plate tectonics began, continuing to the present day.

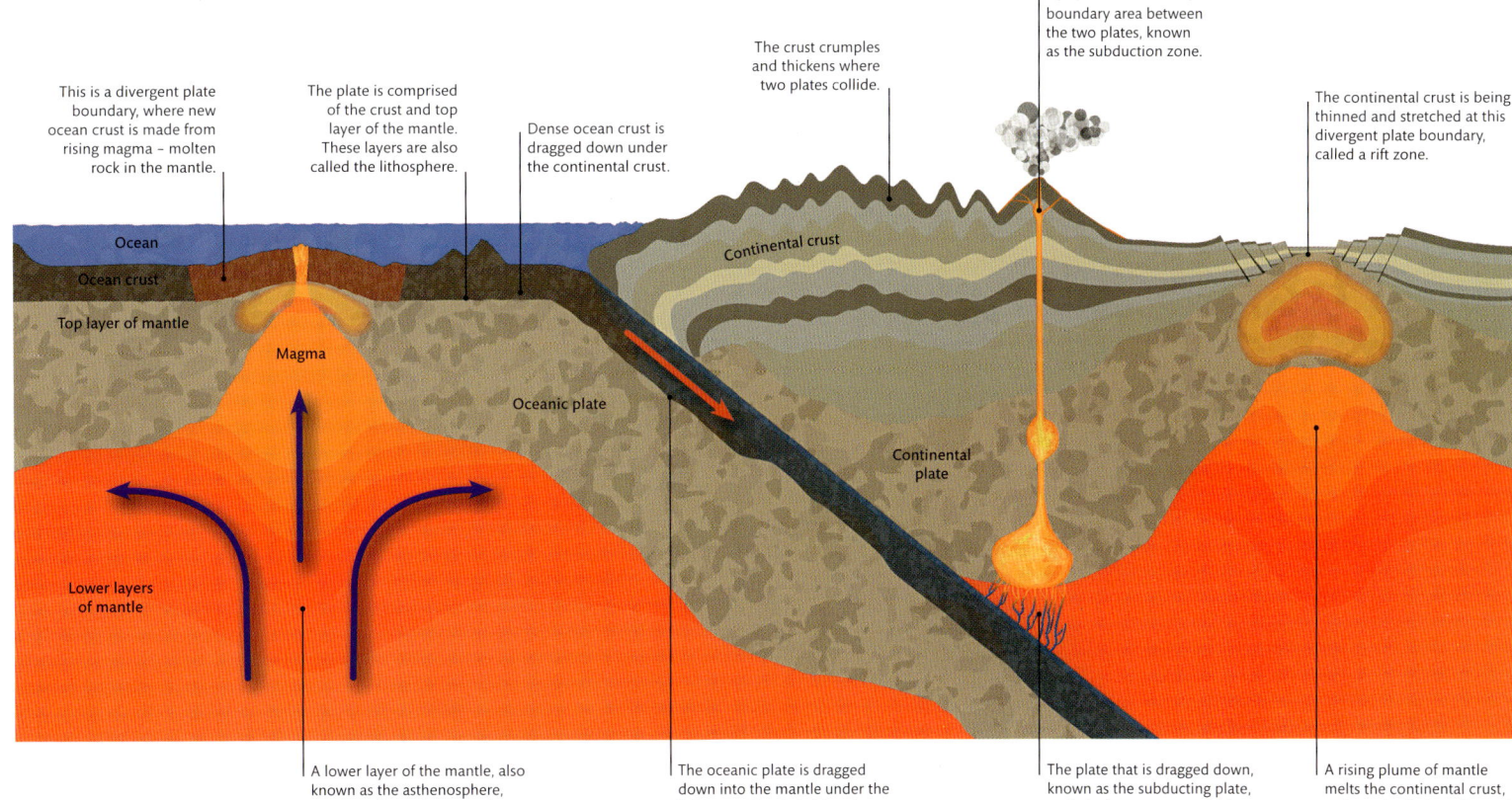

This is a divergent plate boundary, where new ocean crust is made from rising magma – molten rock in the mantle.

The plate is comprised of the crust and top layer of the mantle. These layers are also called the lithosphere.

Dense ocean crust is dragged down under the continental crust.

The crust crumples and thickens where two plates collide.

Volcanoes form above the boundary area between the two plates, known as the subduction zone.

The continental crust is being thinned and stretched at this divergent plate boundary, called a rift zone.

Ocean
Ocean crust
Top layer of mantle
Magma
Oceanic plate
Continental crust
Continental plate
Lower layers of mantle

A lower layer of the mantle, also known as the asthenosphere, consists of hot, viscous rocks. The heat of this magma pushes them up and through the crust.

The oceanic plate is dragged down into the mantle under the lighter continental plate, along with water from the oceans. This is known as subduction.

The plate that is dragged down, known as the subducting plate, melts to form magma, which rises up through cracks to erupt as lava in volcanoes.

A rising plume of mantle melts the continental crust, and eventually tears it apart.

**3.45–2.45 BYA** ARCHAEAN TO PROTEROZOIC EONS

# FIRST LIFE

Slimy mounds of bacteria called stromatolites multiply in the shallow, sunlit seas of the Archaean Eon. These strange, mushroom-shaped life forms use the energy in sunlight, releasing oxygen as a waste product, in a process called photosynthesis. At this time, stromatolites are crucial in generating much of the oxygen in Earth's atmosphere. Today, they are among the oldest known fossils.

**1 Changing skies**
As the atmosphere starts to become richer in oxygen, familiar blue colours replace the fiery red and orange hues of earlier skies. Clouds gather, formed as water vapour emitted from volcanoes condenses.

**2 Early oceans**
Rainfall from condensed water vapour pours down on Earth, filling depressions on the surface and forming the first oceans. It is in water that the earliest organisms evolve, either deep down or in the shallows.

**3 Shallow pools**
Some microbes in these warm, mineral-rich pools use hydrogen sulphide instead of water in their photosynthesis. This generates sulphur instead of oxygen, which leaves yellow stains around the pools.

**4 Stromatolites**
Bizarre colonies of photosynthesizing cyanobacteria (blue-green algae) are held together by sticky slime and particles of sediment. Nearby, dead stromatolites decay, providing food for microbes.

**5 Bubbling away**
Stromatolites release bubbles of oxygen from the water they use in their photosynthesis. The initial rise in oxygen is toxic to most life forms. Many existing organisms die off, leaving space for others to evolve.

**6 Striped rocks**
Oxygen released from the photosynthesizing stromatolites reacts with dissolved iron in the seawater to make solid red iron oxide, or rust. This builds up in bands, alternating with silica-rich bands to give the rocks a striped appearance. These rocks are called Banded Iron Formations.

# ORIGINS OF LIFE

Evidence from fossils suggests life was present on Earth at least 3.7 BYA. Most scientists agree that the first life forms were microscopic, single cells in watery, chemical-rich environments. How they originated remains one of Earth's most puzzling mysteries.

**SUPER CELLS**
For billions of years the only living things on Earth were the simplest single-celled microbes called prokaryotes, such as bacteria. Organisms with more complex cells – called eukaryotes – evolved from these pioneers, and these included plants, animals, and fungi with multicellular bodies.

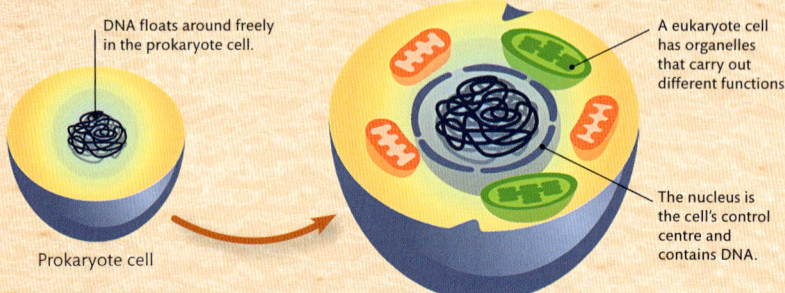

DNA floats around freely in the prokaryote cell.

A eukaryote cell has organelles that carry out different functions.

The nucleus is the cell's control centre and contains DNA.

Prokaryote cell

Eukaryote cell

**Single versus complex cells**
The main difference between these two cells is that the eukaryote has a nucleus, whereas the prokaryote does not.

**WHERE DID LIFE ORIGINATE?**
No one knows exactly where life first began, but the three main theories popular among scientists suggest that life on Earth may have begun in hot springs, in hydrothermal vents under the sea, or even seeded from space on meteorites. All three environments could have allowed complex molecules to form.

**Hot springs**
In warm, shallow pools and springs, the first life forms may have used energy from sunlight to make food through photosynthesis.

Tiny microbes use sunlight and a source of electrons, such as water or hydrogen sulphide, to make food.

**3.7–2.5 BYA: Archaean Eon**
During the Archaean, continents grew from small islands into large landmasses. The first organisms appeared around 04:00. As life evolved, oxygen levels built up in the atmosphere, turning the sky blue.

## THE FIRST PHOTOSYNTHESIZERS

There was no oxygen in Earth's atmosphere to begin with. Tiny microbes called cyanobacteria (blue-green algae) were the first organisms to release oxygen into the air by photosynthesis – the process by which plants, algae, and some bacteria convert carbon dioxide and water into food and oxygen using sunlight. This filled the air with oxygen and led to new species evolving.

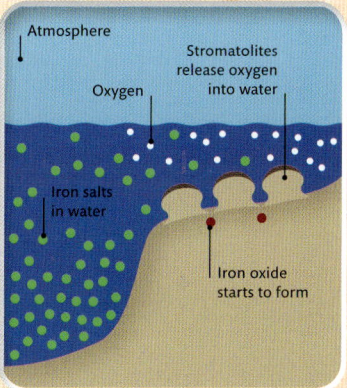

**1 Microbes release oxygen**
Layers of cyanobacteria form rocky mounds called stromatolites. They release oxygen into the water through photosynthesis. The iron salts in the water combine with oxygen to form a solid called iron oxide (rust).

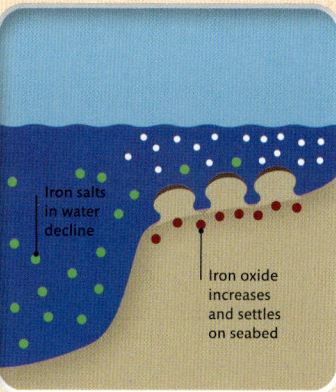

**2 Iron oxide settles on the seafloor**
Oxygen is confined to the water, where it continues to react with iron salts. The layer of iron oxide accumulates and eventually forms a band of iron in the rock.

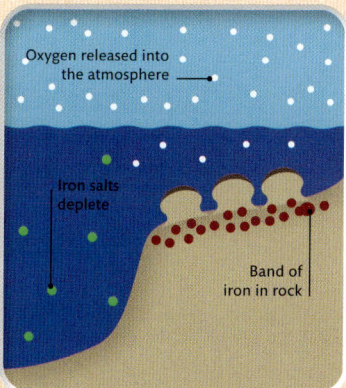

**3 The air fills with oxygen**
As the iron salts in the water deplete, oxygen escapes into the air. The increase in oxygen, initially poisonous to most life, eventually leads to new oxygen-breathing species.

### Hydrothermal vents
In the deep ocean, openings in the seafloor pour out mineral-rich water heated by volcanic activity. The first life forms may have used energy from these reacting minerals to make food – just like some kinds of microbes still living today.

Tiny organisms may have fed on chemicals spewing from the vents.

A meteor on collision with Earth could have seeded the origins of life on Earth.

### Extraterrestrial origin
Another theory, which is less widely accepted, is that the molecules necessary for life were transported to Earth from space by a meteor or comet. If true, this suggests life exists outside Earth, which has not been proven.

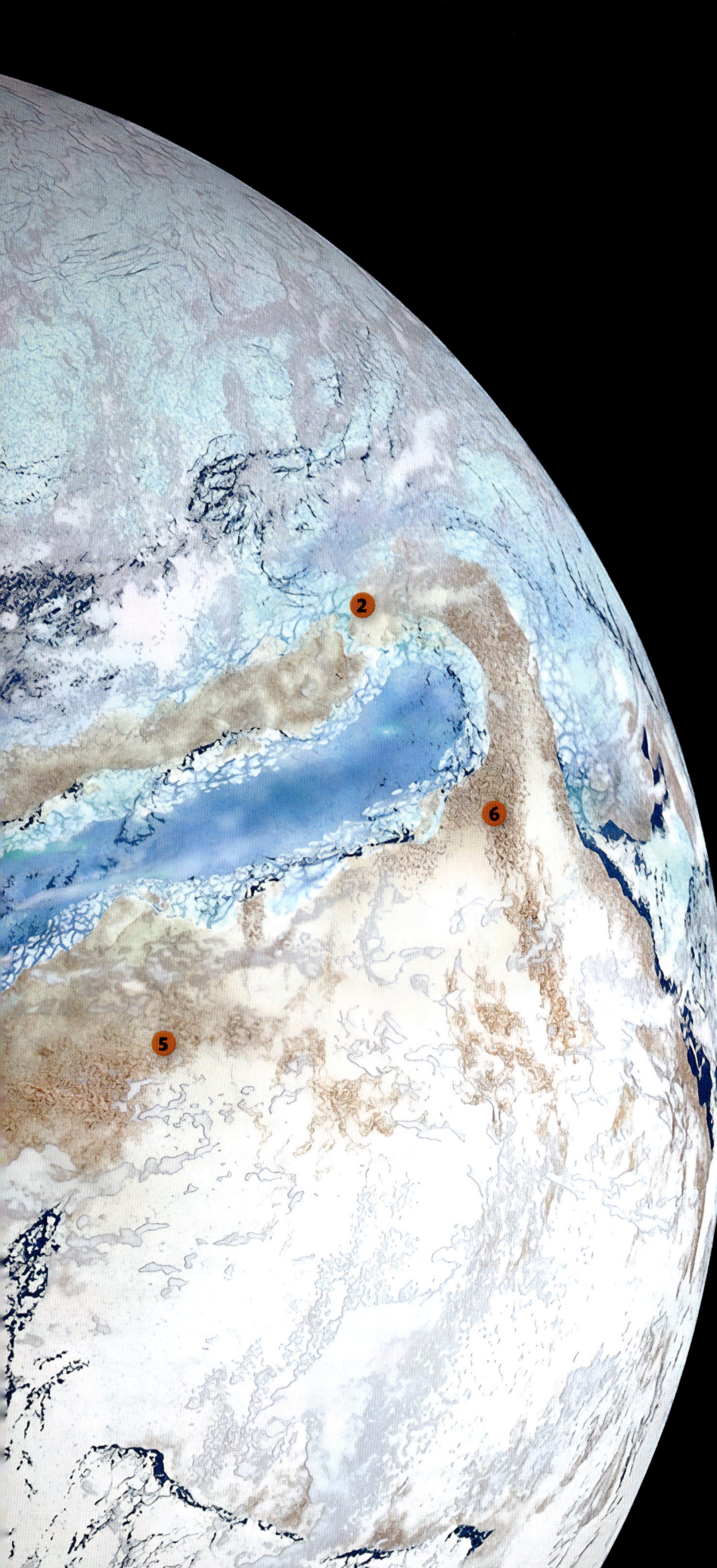

**720–c.635 MYA** PROTEROZOIC EON

# SNOWBALL EARTH

The Proterozoic Eon sees an extreme ice age plunge most of Earth's surface into a frozen world. Yet beneath the icy cover of this giant snowball, multicellular life is evolving in the oceans. Scientists today are still debating the extent of the ice cover and the causes of this dramatic freeze.

### 1 Icy blanket
Though ice cover is probably not continuous and is slushy in places, it is present over most of the land and oceans. With extreme temperatures of -40°C (-40°F), ice sheets may have been up to 800 m (half a mile) thick in places.

### 2 Changing atmosphere
The breakup of supercontinent Rodinia at this time causes limestone to form, which in turn removes carbon dioxide from the atmosphere. The lack of carbon dixoide in the air may have contributed to global cooling, leading to a deep freeze.

### 3 Tropical freeze
Signs of ice discovered in tropical areas near the equator on modern Earth – in the form of sediment carried by melting glaciers during the Proterozoic – provide crucial evidence today for a "Snowball Earth."

### 4 Gluey seawater
In the oceans, multicellular organisms evolve from single-celled organisms, perhaps in response to the increase in cold, viscous seawater. The honey-like consistency of the water makes it difficult for tiny organisms to survive. This may have prompted them to adapt and kickstarted multicellular life.

### 5 Continents under pressure
On land, rocks are squashed and ground up under the immense pressure of thick ice sheets. Some are left with scratch marks made by sharp debris carried at the base of the ice, and others are carried great distances in the moving ice before being deposited.

### 6 Volcanoes
Under the ice or poking out above it, volcanoes pump carbon dioxide into the atmosphere. Massive volcanic eruptions may have allowed the climate to warm and the "Snowball Earth" to thaw.

# THE BIG THAW

The engulfing ice did not last forever. Once Earth heated up enough for the ice to melt, torrents of water poured down from mountains, filling the oceans with nutrients from crushed rock. The stage was set for the evolution of complex life.

**THE RISE OF ALGAE**
Slime, consisting of bacteria and other single-celled organisms, dominated the Earth for about 2.5 billion years. The surge in nutrient-rich meltwaters may have allowed multicellular algae to diversify.

**Weathering**
The loosening of rocks by moving ice allowed nutrients from continental rocks to be transported to the oceans.

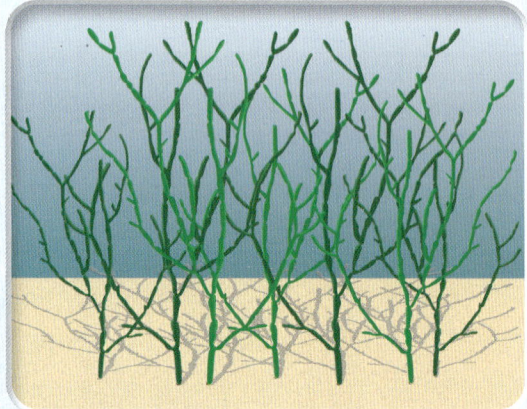

**EARLY SEAWEEDS**
Fossil evidence shows that billion-year-old seaweeds had multiple thin branches and root-like anchoring structures. These multicellular seaweeds were among the earliest complex organisms to evolve.

**ICE DETECTIVES**
When a mass of ice moves over rocks it leaves behind scratch marks like the ones above. Geologists use this evidence to prove where and how ancient glaciers and ice sheets moved.

**Multicellular algae**
Some multicellular algae contained green chlorophyll, while others had red pigments to help absorb light at different depths.

# AN EXPLOSION OF LIFE

**Trilobites**
For more than 250 million years, the oceans were teeming with trilobites – early arthropods. Their segmented bodies make for some of the most distinctive fossils found in rocks.

**560-550 MYA** EDIACARAN PERIOD

# THE FIRST ANIMALS

Below the waves that rage through the surface waters of the Ediacaran Period, bizarre-looking, mostly soft-bodied creatures lurk on the ocean floor. Made up of different types of cells, they consume food from their environment, which makes them the first known animals.

**1 Seafloor forests**
Mysterious, feathery, frond-like creatures form forests on the seafloor. Anchored to the bottom by root-like structures called holdfasts, these marine animals work together, absorbing nutrients from the waters.

**2 Tubular animals**
Rope-like organisms colonize the seafloor, forming closely-packed groups of individuals of similar sizes. These animals, called *Funisia*, may have been filter-feeders, like modern-day sponges.

**3 Primitive brain**
Sensing that food is nearby, *Spriggina* crawls towards it. Behind its horseshoe-shaped head lies what may be one of the earliest brains in the animal kingdom.

**4 Slug-like grazer**
*Kimberella*, which may be a primitive mollusc, stretches forward to scratch and feed off microbial mats – layers of bacteria and algae – on the seafloor.

**5 Burrows**
Worm-like animals burrow into the seabed, stirring up sediment. This helps to oxygenate the mud and add nutrients to the water.

**6 Anchored animal**
Fixed in place, *Tribrachidium* is feeding on tiny particles suspended in the water. Three arm-like structures form a spiral pattern on this curious, dome-shaped organism.

**7 Saucer-shaped creature**
*Dickinsonia*, a flat, disc-shaped animal with prominent rib-like structures extending out from a central line, is grazing on mats of microbes.

# CURIOUS CREATURES

Forty million years before the explosion of animal life as we know it, in the Ediacaran, communities of strange-looking multicelled organisms thrived on the seafloor. Despite their appearance, these early animals had some characteristics similar to modern animals. Many probably consumed food from their surroundings and even moved about.

**DISCOVERING FOSSILS**
The only information we have on very early animals comes from fossils excavated by palaeontologists. Most fossils only preserve the hard parts of organisms, so soft-bodied fossils such as those of Ediacaran Period creatures are very rare. Unearthing delicate fossils is a slow process and palaeontologists must work carefully, using special tools.

The identity of the animals that lived inside the tubes is still a mystery, but fossils indicate that they had guts.

Three arms curved out from the centre, perhaps helping to funnel currents, and food, towards itself.

**DIVERSE LIFEFORMS**
From flat discs to tiny cones, feathery quills, and rugby balls, the earliest animal communities evolved a remarkable diversity of shape, size, and symmetry. They also had muscle tissues, hard skeletons, and groups of cells with specialized tasks.

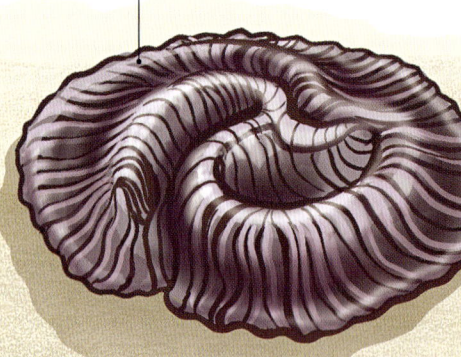

This organism had radial symmetry – it could be divided into equal parts by slicing through its centre in any direction.

**Tribrachidium**
This bizarre, dome-shaped creature was 5 cm (2 in) in diameter and had tri-radial symmetry, meaning it had three identical body parts radiating from its core.

**Cyclomedusa**
Initially thought to be a floating jellyfish, this mysterious disc-shaped creature probably rested on the seabed.

**Cloudina**
Possibly the first shells, these small, stacked, calcite tubes were ancient reef builders.

Fossils show that *Spriggina's* body was made of segments.

**560–550 mya: Ediacaran Period**
After "Snowball Earth" thawed around 21:00, oxygen levels built up in the air and oceans. As the giant continent Rodinia broke up, shallow seas formed, becoming home to early animals.

**Spriggina**
Thought to be an early arthropod or a worm, this creature's body was divided into mirror-image halves, making it one of the earliest examples of bilateral symmetry.

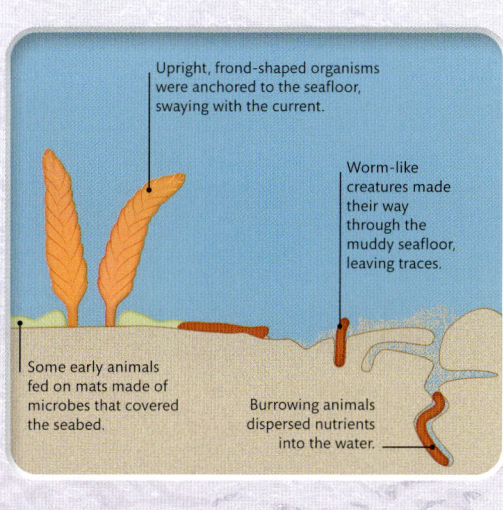

**MOVEMENT ON THE SEAFLOOR**
From wriggling and crawling to burrowing and slithering, the first animals had different ways of getting around the seafloor. These movements stirred up nutrients from the bottom into the water, feeding other creatures.

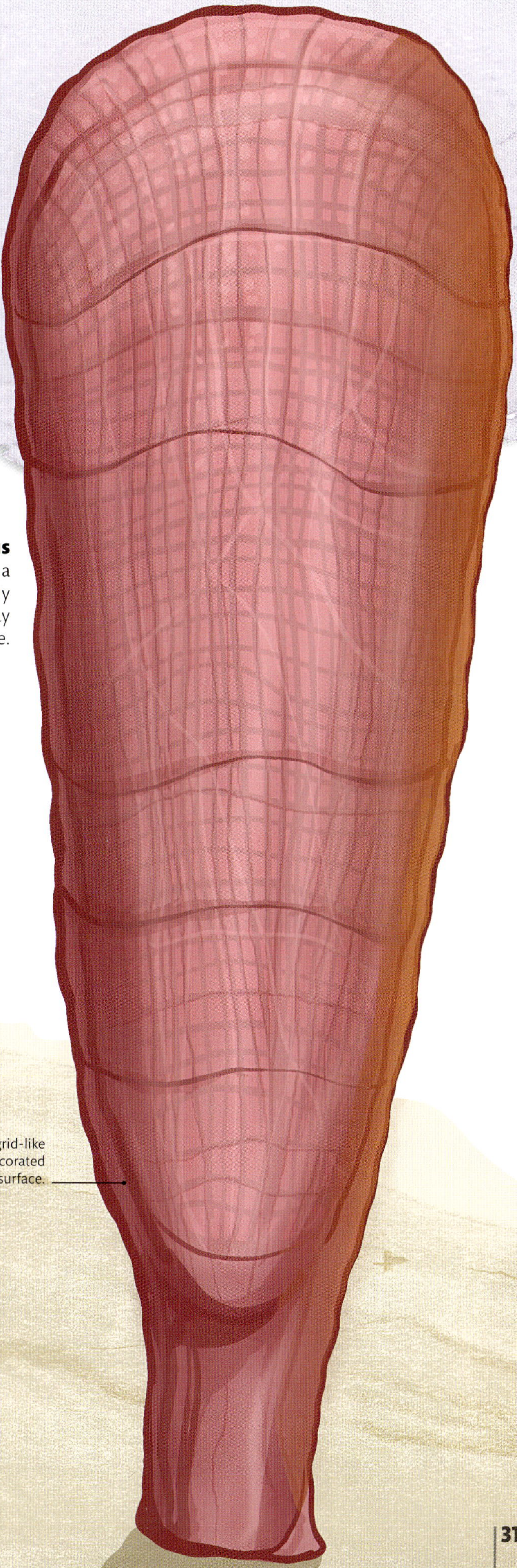

Upright, frond-shaped organisms were anchored to the seafloor, swaying with the current.

Worm-like creatures made their way through the muddy seafloor, leaving traces.

Some early animals fed on mats made of microbes that covered the seabed.

Burrowing animals dispersed nutrients into the water.

Currents entered the hollows inside the organisms, where nutrients were filtered out as the water passed through.

**Helicolocellus**
This ancient sponge had a goblet-shaped, conical body with radial symmetry and may have been hollow inside.

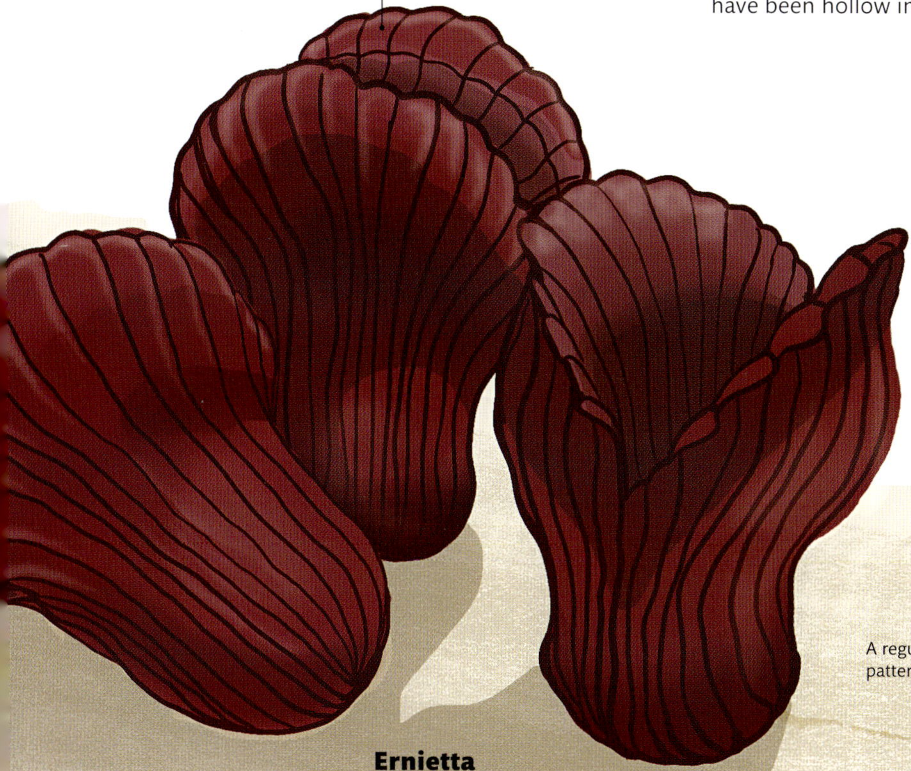

A regular grid-like pattern decorated the surface.

**Ernietta**
This fan-shaped, sack-like organism lived in groups on the seafloor, probably filtering food particles from the water.

**Size comparison**

**c.540–500 MYA** CAMBRIAN PERIOD

# LIFE EXPLODES

Suddenly, in the Cambrian Period, life diversifies into a wonderful variety of soft- and hard-bodied organisms. The so-called "Cambrian Explosion" sees the emergence of complex animals, including the ancestors of most major animal groups we recognise today.

**1 Five-eyed arthropod**
*Opabinia* is a fearsome predator of the Cambrian oceans. Its long appendage or proboscis is equipped with a claw for seizing soft prey.

**2 Apex predator**
Lurking in the distance is *Anomalocaris*, another predator that can chase and catch prey with its flexible, spiked mouthparts.

**3 Armoured slug**
This ancient slug, called *Wiwaxia*, is covered in scales and has two rows of spines on its back to deter predators.

**4 Bristle worm**
This alien-like creature scours the ocean floor for mud, using its two tentacles. Paired bundles of bristles decorate its body.

**5 Pointy prickles**
*Hallucigenia*, named after its surreal appearance, has spikes lining its back and walks around on flexible legs, each terminating in a pair of claws.

**6 Spiny swimmer**
Sporting a head shield made of two backward pointing spines, *Marrella* swims close to the seabed, periodically resting on its appendages.

**7 Primitive fish**
*Pikaia's* body has a supporting rod that works like a primitive backbone. It probably uses its gill slits to filter food – not for breathing, like modern fishes.

**8 Ancient sponges**
Attached to the seafloor, sponge *Vauxia* extracts food particles from water passing through its walls. Its cone-shaped skeleton has two layers.

# POWER GRAB

The burst of evolutionary change in the Cambrian Period saw animals grow in size and become more diverse and complex. These creatures left their mark in the rocks of famous fossil sites such as the Burgess Shale in Canada. Here, sudden underwater mudslides buried organisms, sealing their fate as fossils and giving us clues about how they lived.

## MONSTER SHRIMP

From the Greek word for "odd shrimp", *Anomalocaris* was a giant arthropod cruising the Cambrian seas in search of prey. Growing up to 40 cm (16 in) long, it may have been the first large hunter on Earth. Fossils of this top predator have been found in the USA, Canada, China, and Australia.

**Powerful eyes**
Large eyes on top of stalks were made of many tiny lenses, providing excellent vision.

**Grasping weapons**
Two spiny limbs on the head could snatch soft prey – a bit like the front legs of a praying mantis.

**Vicious spines**
Spines helped to grip prey before it was swept into the mouth under the head.

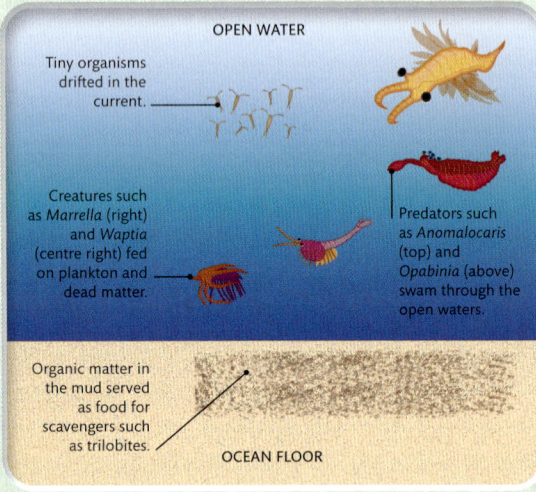

OPEN WATER
Tiny organisms drifted in the current.
Creatures such as *Marrella* (right) and *Waptia* (centre right) fed on plankton and dead matter.
Predators such as *Anomalocaris* (top) and *Opabinia* (above) swam through the open waters.
Organic matter in the mud served as food for scavengers such as trilobites.
OCEAN FLOOR

## FILLING THE OCEAN'S LAYERS
In the Cambrian seas, some animals drifted in the current, while others swam in the open waters, or crawled and scavenged on the seafloor looking for food.

## ANCIENT SHELLS
Trilobites – arthropods with armoured skeletons – first appeared in the Cambrian Period alongside many other animals with hard shells. Their fossils have been found all over the world.

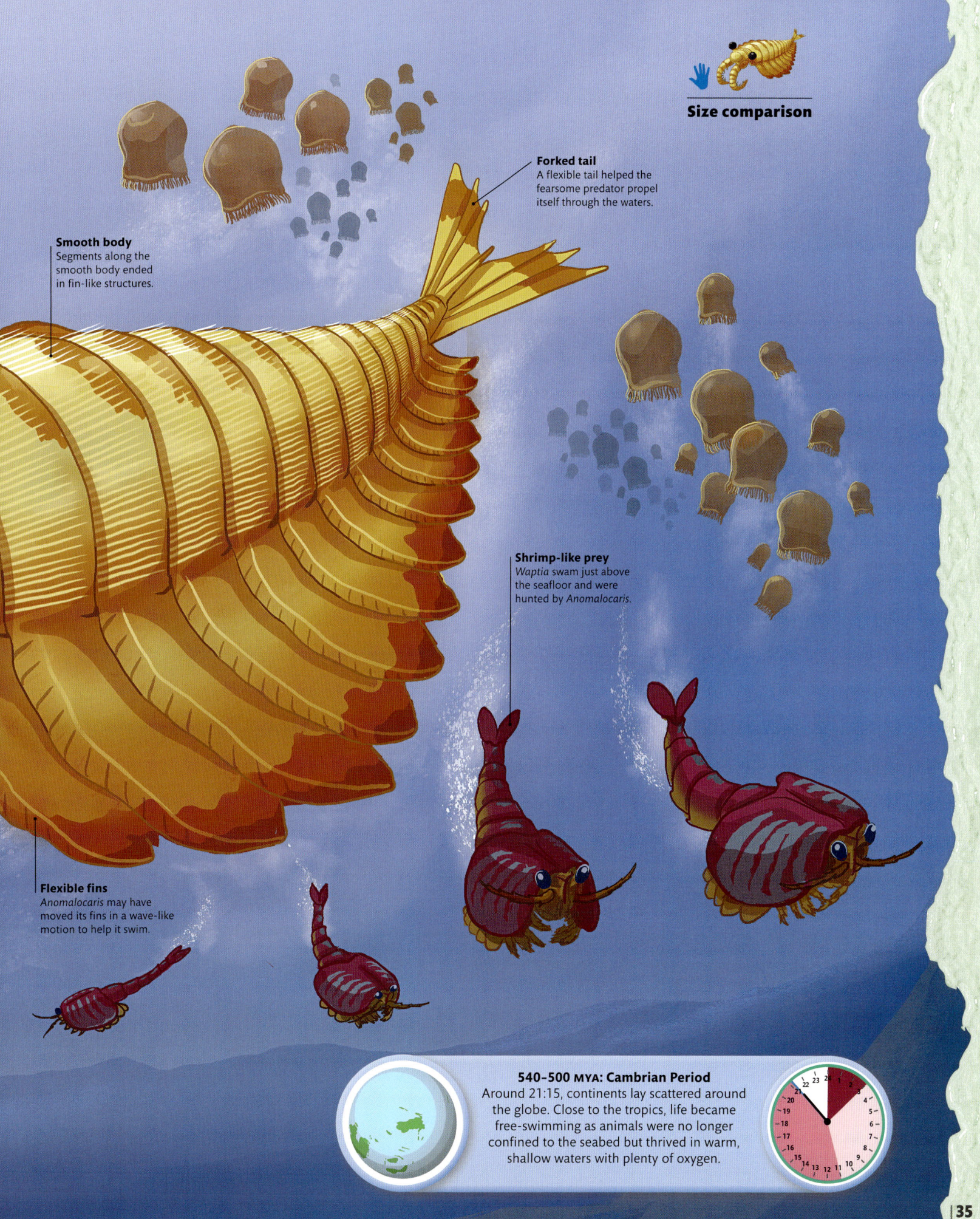

**407 MYA** DEVONIAN PERIOD

# GREENING THE LAND

Among the hot springs and geysers of the Devonian Period, some of the earliest land plants grow in the damp ground, providing cover for tiny, insect-like creatures. These plant pioneers are less than 40 cm (16 in) in height and resemble today's mosses.

**1 Early club moss**
Decorated by leaf-like scales in spirals around the stem, *Asteroxylon* is an early vascular plant. This means it has the ability to transport water and nutrients along its stem, in tubes. In this plant, the tubes are star-shaped.

**2 Porous stems**
Pores called stomata help *Aglaophyton* and other plants adapt to life on land. Carbon dioxide from the air enters the plant for photosynthesis and water drawn up from the soil evaporates through the stomata.

**3 Towering mushrooms**
Rising high above the landscape are peculiar pillars called *Prototaxites*. Reaching 8 m (26 ft) in height, these organisms may be plant-like fungi or lichens.

**4 Bristly springtail**
Antennae emerge from the inflated body of *Rhyniella*, a many-legged relative of insects. Sensing danger, it gets ready to catapult itself into the air like a spring.

**5 Spore-bearing capsules**
*Rhynia's* spores, safely tucked inside oval capsules, enable it to reproduce. Dispersed in the air rather than in water, they are resistant to drying out.

**6 Supportive stems**
A strong tissue structure allows *Sciadophyton's* simple stems to stay upright without collapsing. Cups at the top of the stems contain male and female cells.

**7 Spider-like predator**
Hairy-legged *Palaeocharinus* senses that prey is nearby. Arthropods – invertebrates with hard outer skeletons and jointed legs, such as *Palaeocharinus* – are among the earliest animals to thrive on land.

**8 Fungal roots**
Tiny fungi living inside its roots help *Horneophyton* absorb minerals. In return, they receive some of the plant's sugars. Symbiotic relationships like this are still common in today's plants.

# FORESTS EMERGE

Up until the Ordovician Period, the land was barren, except for slime-like algae and perhaps lichen encrusting rocks. But once land plants became well established in the Devonian Period, it only took a few tens of millions of years for tall forests to evolve.

**EARLY VASCULAR PLANTS**
Vascular plants such as *Aglaophyton* (above) have tiny pipes running through their stems that transport water and minerals from the ground upwards and help them grow tall. But the earliest, such as *Cooksonia*, grew no taller than 30 cm (12 in).

**FISH DIVERSIFY**
By the Devonian Period, bony fishes were diversifying in two main groups. Lobe-finned fish, such as the coelacanth (above), have fleshy, limb-like fins. Ray-finned fish, which include most modern fish such as eels (below), have thin radiating bones in their fins.

**WOODY PIONEERS**
Transport pipes in many plants evolved into wood, which gave them the strength to grow taller and escape the shade of their neighbours. This helped their leaves reach more light for photosynthesis.

**Devonian giant**
*Archaeopteris* could grow 30 m (98 ft) tall, with a trunk over 1 m (3 ft) wide.

**Stabilizing roots**
Roots helped plants reach more water and minerals in the ground, and also anchored their growing weight.

**Millipede**
Thriving in the undergrowth, creepy-crawlies such as millipedes would feast on dead plant matter.

c.385–375 MYA DEVONIAN PERIOD

# FISH OUT OF WATER

Hot, humid air rises up from shallow, freshwater swamps. The first four-legged vertebrates, called tetrapods, venture out of the water, leaving footprints in the mud. These tentative first steps in the Devonian Period mark the transition of some vertebrates from water to land, leading all the way to humans millions of years later.

### 1 Fishapod
Descended from lobe-finned fishes, *Tiktaalik* is a fish with features of early tetrapods. Up to 3 m (9 ft) long, it uses strong, paddle-like fins, which work like limbs, to crawl onto the muddy bank.

### 2 Lobe-finned fish
Hunting nearby is a coelacanth, a lobe-finned fish. It was long thought to have become extinct in the Cretaceous Period, before being discovered alive in 1938 off the coast of South Africa.

### 3 Skeletal support
*Tiktaalik* has a blend of land and water adaptations, including its bony fins. This freshwater creature's robust rib cage and bone structure help support its weight when moving outside the water.

### 4 Riverbed nursery
Early tetrapods, like modern amphibians, lay their eggs in water. The newly-hatched *Tiktaalik* larvae, called tadpoles, use gills to breathe in water before transforming into their adult form, with lungs.

### 5 Coming up for air
Among its terrestrial adaptations, *Tiktaalik*'s lungs allow it to breathe in gulps of warm air. This adaptation coexists with internal gills, which it uses for breathing when in water.

### 6 Powerful hips
Long back fins, a large pelvis, and prominent hip joints help *Tiktaalik* prop itself upright either on the riverbed or to make the first forays onto land.

### 7 Ray-finned fish
Like most fish, the predatory *Cheirolepis* has fins supported by bony rays to help with swimming, and breathes underwater by using gills to absorb oxygen.

# HOW FOSSILS FORM

When most organisms die, they decay and leave no trace. However, in special circumstances dead life forms can end up preserved in rocks as fossils. For this to happen, they must be buried rapidly in sediment before they decay.

**TRAILBLAZING TETRAPODS**
The first four-limbed, backboned animals to walk on land evolved from swimming fishes. The evolution of these tetrapods in the Devonian Period can be traced through fossils in the rock record – layers of rock that provide clues about Earth's history.

**INDEX FOSSILS**
Organisms that exist for many millions of years have so-called long ranges. More short-lived organisms have shorter ranges. Known as index fossils, these short-lived organisms provide useful clues about the age of rocks they are found in.

**Poor index fossil**
This type of brachiopod existed for a long time, so it is little use as an index fossil.

## BURIED IN TIME
From bones to footprints, fossils tell a tale of changing environments and evolution. There are many stages involved in fossilization and the process takes tens of thousands or even millions of years.

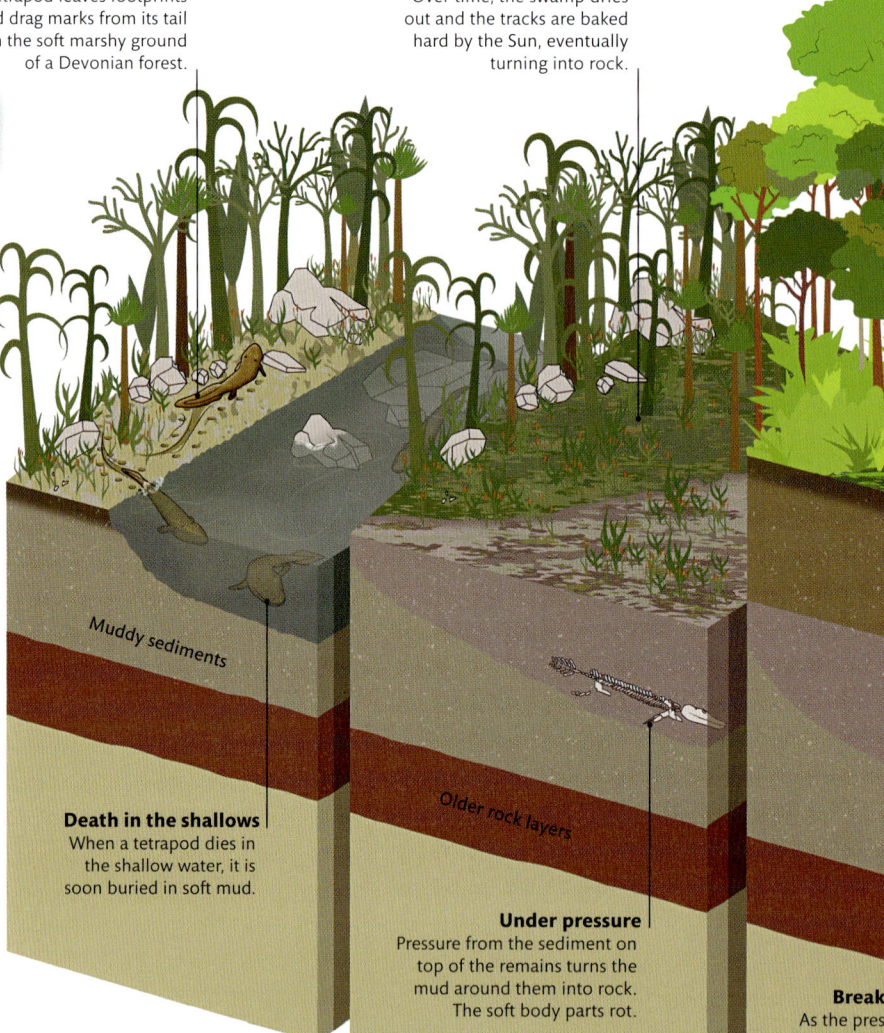

**Life in the forest**
A tetrapod leaves footprints and drag marks from its tail on the soft marshy ground of a Devonian forest.

**Passage of time**
Over time, the swamp dries out and the tracks are baked hard by the Sun, eventually turning into rock.

**New growth**
Sediment continues to build up. Millions of years later, trees grow taller and larger. The forest is home to new organisms.

**Death in the shallows**
When a tetrapod dies in the shallow water, it is soon buried in soft mud.

**Under pressure**
Pressure from the sediment on top of the remains turns the mud around them into rock. The soft body parts rot.

**Breaking up**
As the pressure of accumulated sediment increases, the bones of the tetrapod's body may break apart.

**Good index fossil**
This type of trilobite only lived in part of the Cambrian Period, making it a useful index fossil.

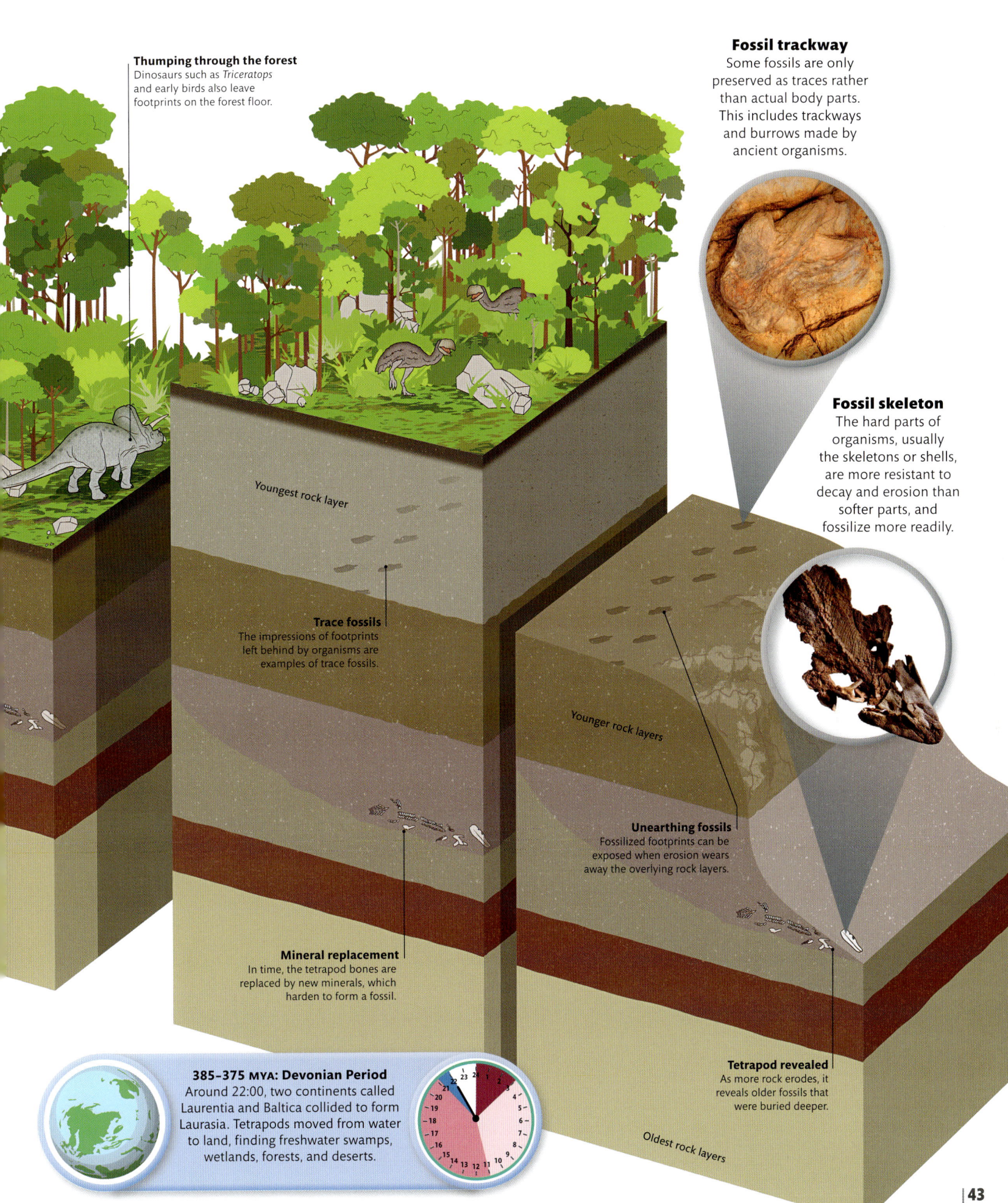

c.325–318 MYA **CARBONIFEROUS PERIOD**

# TROPICAL OCEANS

Near the edge of a humid, swampy forest, a warm Sun sets over shallow, tropical waters. From bizarre sharks to reef-building corals and spiral-shelled molluscs, the Carboniferous seas are teeming with life.

### 1 Swampy forest
On land, forested swamps occupy low-lying areas. Here, colossal trees can grow as tall as 50 m (164 ft), around the height of a 15-storey building.

### 2 Giant shark
This large predator, called *Glikmanius*, can grow over 6 m (20 ft) long. They are just one of many types of shark to evolve at this time.

### 3 Coiled creatures
Spiral-shelled molluscs called ammonoids steer their way through the waters, using their tentacles to capture and direct prey to their jaws, where it is shredded alive.

### 4 Angel-winged shells
Brachiopods are marine organisms with hinged shells that look like angel wings. They stay on the seafloor, anchored by spines, and have tiny anemone-like rings of tentacles for catching food.

### 5 Dancing sea lilies
Sea lilies called crinoids wave their arms in the currents, drawing in food particles. Related to sea urchins, but with stalks, they form forests on the seabed.

### 6 Peculiar fins
A school of male sharks called *Stethacanthus* glide along sporting odd-shaped dorsal fins and crests covered in tooth-like structures. These may help them attract and grasp females.

### 7 Colonial corals
Living together in balloon-like colonies on the seafloor, individual corals called polyps form hard skeletons of calcium carbonate that support the colony.

### 8 Ocean vacuum cleaner
Snails with coiled shells called gastropods graze the ocean floor using a sharp tongue to lick and scrape off seaweed and other detritus from rocks and sediment.

# CARBON SWAMPS

The Late Carboniferous Period was a time of giants. Plants and animals grew in size and massive rivers carried mud, silt, and sand into the seas. Vast swamp forests flourished that would eventually decay and become the coal deposits that give the Carboniferous its name, which means "coal bearing".

**Size comparison**

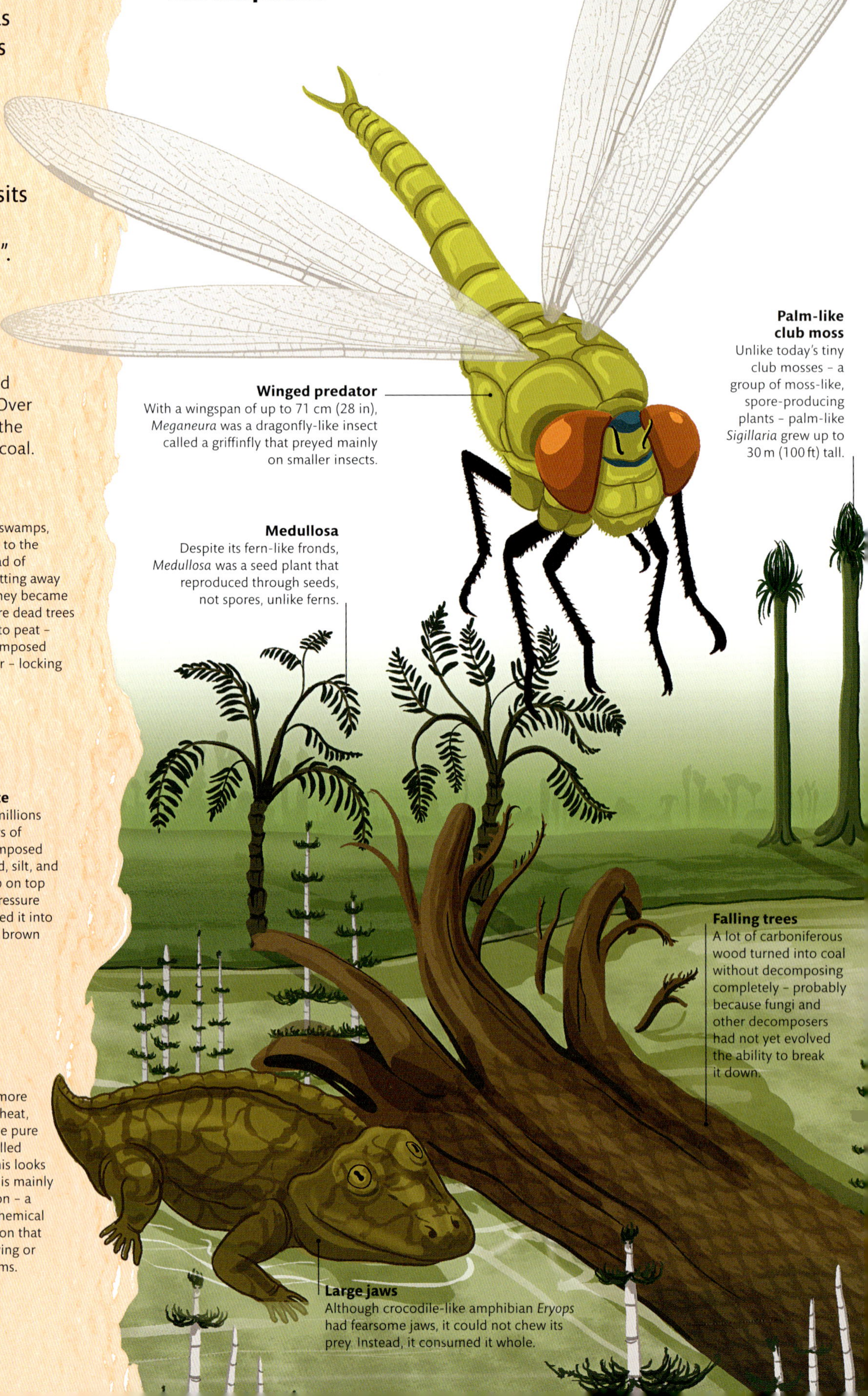

## HOW COAL WAS FORMED
In the densely forested swamps, dead vegetation accumulated. This partially decayed in the bogs, turning into carbon-rich peat. Over millions of years, heat and pressure turned the peat into lignite and, eventually, anthracite coal.

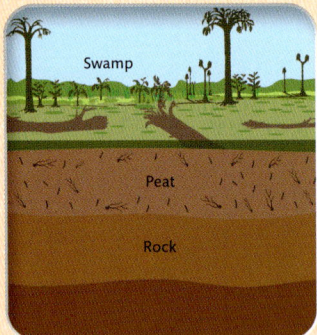

**1 Peat**
In the swamps, dead trees fell to the ground. Instead of completely rotting away underwater, they became buried by more dead trees and turned into peat – partially decomposed organic matter – locking away carbon.

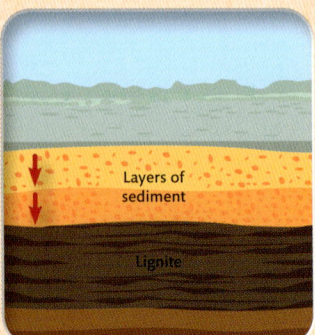

**2 Lignite**
Over millions of years, layers of sediment, composed mainly of mud, silt, and sand, piled up on top of the peat. Pressure and heat turned it into lignite, a soft, brown form of coal.

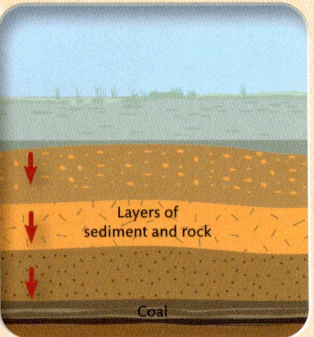

**3 Coal**
With more pressure and heat, lignite became pure black coal, called anthracite. This looks like rock, but is mainly organic carbon – a form of the chemical element carbon that is found in living or dead organisms.

**Winged predator**
With a wingspan of up to 71 cm (28 in), *Meganeura* was a dragonfly-like insect called a griffinfly that preyed mainly on smaller insects.

**Medullosa**
Despite its fern-like fronds, *Medullosa* was a seed plant that reproduced through seeds, not spores, unlike ferns.

**Palm-like club moss**
Unlike today's tiny club mosses – a group of moss-like, spore-producing plants – palm-like *Sigillaria* grew up to 30 m (100 ft) tall.

**Falling trees**
A lot of carboniferous wood turned into coal without decomposing completely – probably because fungi and other decomposers had not yet evolved the ability to break it down.

**Large jaws**
Although crocodile-like amphibian *Eryops* had fearsome jaws, it could not chew its prey. Instead, it consumed it whole.

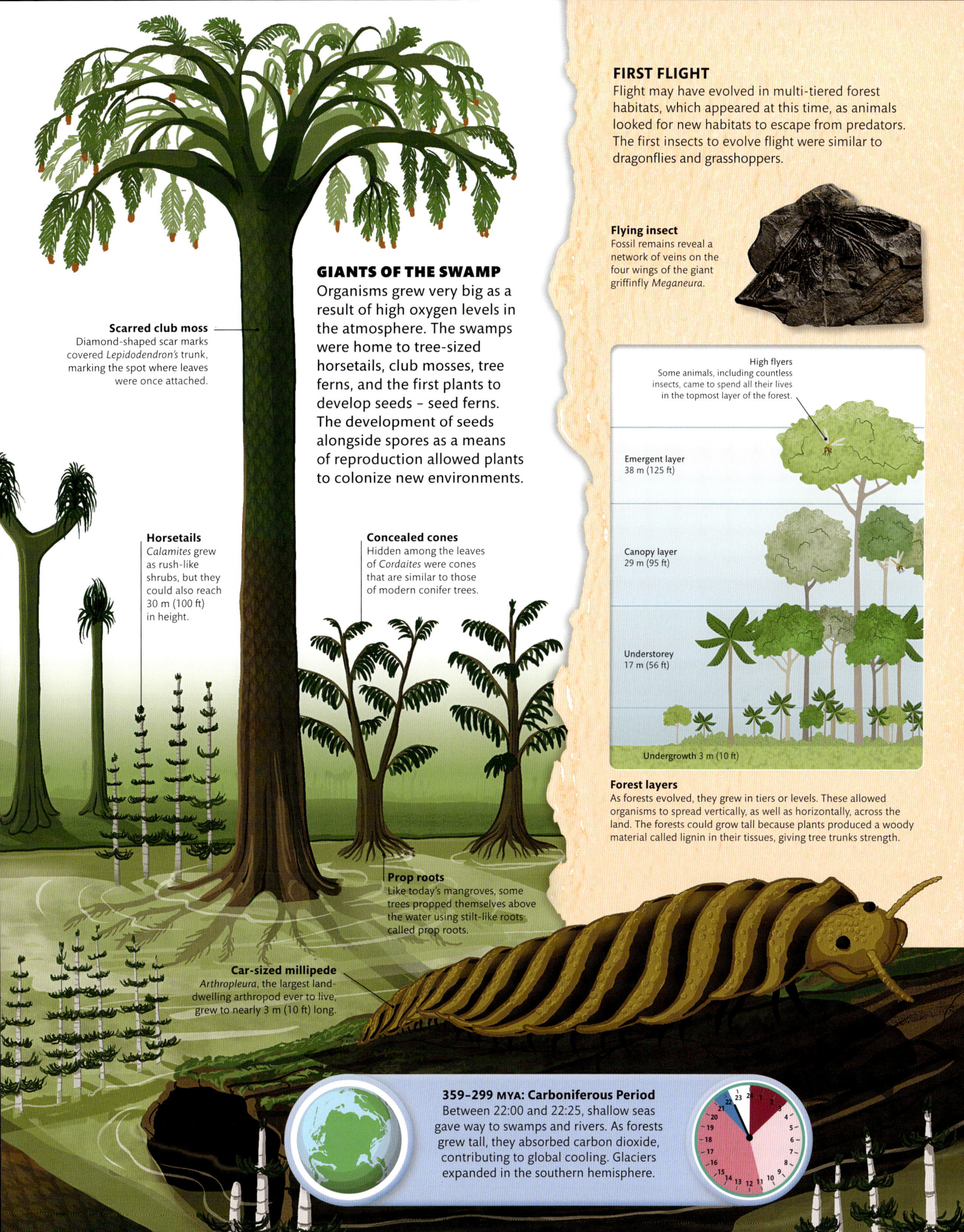

**252 MYA** LATE PERMIAN PERIOD

# THE GREAT DYING

In the Late Permian Period, the sky grows dark, torrents of lava engulf everything in their path, and the ocean becomes a toxic soup. Up to 95 per cent of species go extinct, including most vertebrates on land. Preceded by a smaller extinction event, this is the biggest extinction of all time.

**① Catastrophic eruptions**
Massive volcanic eruptions in Siberia spew out 2 million sq km (780,000 sq miles) of deadly lava. They release carbon dioxide, causing global warming, and plumes of sulphur and ash that turn the sky dark.

**② Stranded on land**
When supercontinent Pangaea formed in the Early Permian Period, the coastline decreased and marine organisms fell. They now suffer even greater losses.

**③ The last meal**
In Pangaea's arid interior, reptiles are well-adapted to the dry conditions. *Inostrancevia*, a sabre-toothed carnivore, scavenges for stranded carcasses. It is a gorgonopsian – an early ancestor of modern mammals.

**④ Rhino-sized reptile**
This pareiasaur, an armoured herbivore, is caught between approaching lava flows and hungry gorgonopsian predators. Pareiasaurs and gorgonopsians are among the 70 per cent of land vertebrate families that are wiped out at this time.

**⑤ Corals in trouble**
As the oceans become acidic and lacking in oxygen, horn-shaped, wrinkly rugose corals and tabulate corals, with hard horizontal plates, die out.

**⑥ Future fossils**
Unable to survive the toxic water, ammonites eventually all but disappear. Spiral shells on the seabed are all that is left of these marine molluscs after their death.

**⑦ Trilobite flurry**
Trilobites scurry away to no avail, for they are among the organisms about to become extinct. Other marine creatures such as brachiopods, bryozoans, and crinoids are severely reduced.

# MASS EXTINCTIONS

Life on Earth is able to adapt to gradual changes in the environment, but sudden shifts can be devastating. Earth's history includes volcanic eruptions lasting millions of years, tsunamis taller than skyscrapers, rapid climate change, and a massive asteroid impact. The worst of these have led to most species on the planet dying out – mass extinctions.

### VOLCANIC EFFECTS
Mass extinctions often coincide with prolonged, massive volcanic eruptions. Their effects can be devastating for life, as gases and dust block out the Sun, which restricts photosynthesis, while greenhouse gas emissions cause severe global warming.

### BIG FIVE, PLUS ONE
We know of five mass extinctions in Earth's history. This chart shows them and uses fossil records to track the number of different families of sea creatures through time. It shows not only how numbers dropped, but also how fast new groups replaced them.

**252 MYA: Late Permian Period**
The Great Dying took place at 22:40 on our 24-hour clock. At this time, the supercontinent Pangaea, meaning "all lands", stretched almost from pole to pole, surrounded by a single vast ocean called Panthalassa.

The diversity of life rose dramatically during the Ordovician.

Marine life recovered during the Silurian.

During the Carboniferous, life diversified in the oceans and on land.

Total families of sea creatures

CAMBRIAN | ORDOVICIAN | SILURIAN | DEVONIAN | CARBONIFEROUS

Geological time period

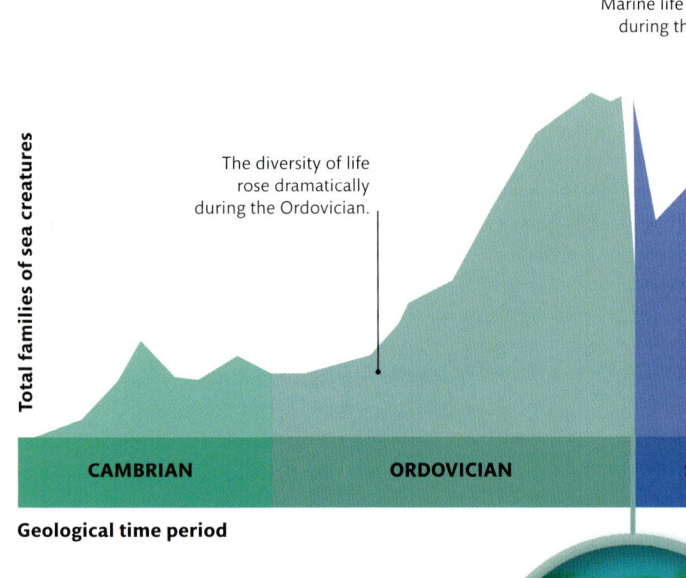

**Late Ordovician, 443 MYA**
Global cooling led to huge glaciers forming. This lowered sea levels, reducing underwater habitats. Bizarre marine invertebrates called graptolites were severely affected.

*86% of species lost*

**Late Devonian, 374 MYA**
Global cooling, habitat loss, and algal blooms may have caused this extinction. Marine reefs were hit hard, and placoderm fish died out entirely.

*75% of species lost*

50

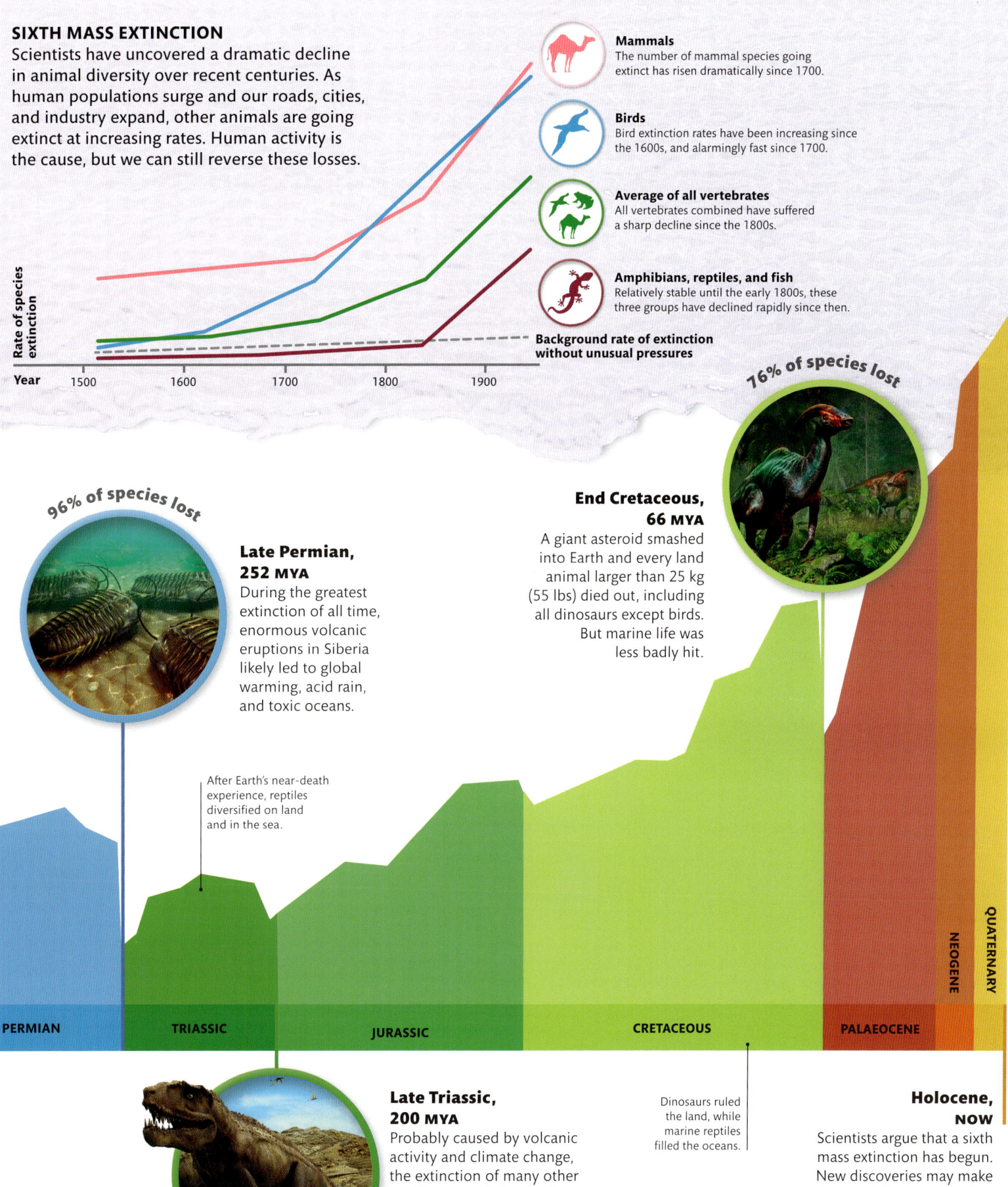

# THE RISE OF DINOSAURS

**Dinosaur world**
A pair of *Eotriceratops* stand alongside an *Edmontosaurus*. These dinosaurs once roamed an area of what is now North America.

**165–163 MYA** JURASSIC PERIOD

# JURASSIC SEAS

After the Triassic mass extinction 200 MYA, life in the seas has recovered. Monstrous marine reptiles descended from lizard-like terrestrial ancestors fill the oceans. Now well-adapted to an aquatic lifestyle, they hunt underwater prey such as fish and molluscs, surface to breathe, and, in some cases, even give birth to their young in the water.

**❶ Giant bony-fish**
Despite being armed with over 40,000 teeth, this gentle *Leedsichthys* glides peacefully through the water, filtering tasty morsels of plankton using its massive, basket-shaped mouth.

**❷ Monstrous pliosaur**
*Liopleurodon* is 7 m (23 ft) long and has razor-sharp teeth and powerful paddles. Taking advantage of a plesiosaur's moment of distraction, it ambushes the unsuspecting prey.

**❸ Dart-shaped belemnites**
With soft bodies around a bullet-shaped internal shell, these squid-like molluscs are equipped with ten arms, each terminating in sharp hooks for grasping prey.

**❹ Fleeing plesiosaur**
This dragon-like reptile jerks its long neck away from *Liopleurodon*'s powerful jaws, waving its paddles up and down to flee, as it carries its own ammonite prey.

**❺ Fish lizard**
A pregnant ichthyosaur prepares to give birth to live young in the water while older offspring follow nearby. Ichthyosaurs, which means "fish lizards", are well adapted to an aquatic lifestyle.

**❻ Spiral-shaped ammonites**
Partly protected by their ornate shells, these molluscs expel jets of water from their bodies in an attempt to propel themselves away from danger.

**❼ Ancient shark**
Lurking in the dark, *Hybodus* is searching for belemnite prey. It has sharp front teeth for grabbing and rounded back teeth for crushing its victims, giving it its name, which means "humped tooth".

# AMMONITES

The Jurassic seas teemed with ammonites, now-extinct molluscs whose modern relatives, such as octopus and squid, have advanced brains and complex nervous systems. Their coiled shells are commonly found in Jurassic rock, and they lived throughout the Cretaceous Period, too.

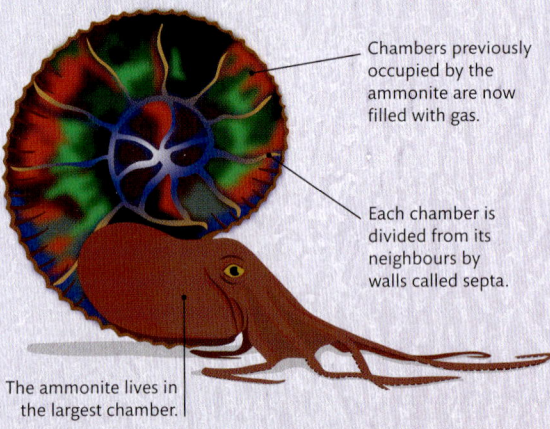

Chambers previously occupied by the ammonite are now filled with gas.

Each chamber is divided from its neighbours by walls called septa.

The ammonite lives in the largest chamber.

**BUILDING A NEW HOME**
There were many chambers inside an ammonite shell, but the soft-bodied animal only occupied one at a time. As it grew too large for each chamber, it built a new one, slowly forming a spiral.

**AMMONITE FOSSIL**
This fossil has been cut in half, revealing the empty chambers within the shell have been filled by pale minerals that form crystals.

**Seizing prey**
Behind the tentacles used to capture prey were strong jaws to shred and eat it.

**External shell**
The tough external shell was usually covered in ridges, bumps, and spines.

**Jet propulsion**
Ammonites moved by expelling jets of water away from their body to propel themselves in the opposite direction.

**Wavy suture lines**
These wavy lines, revealed when the external shell is removed, mark the contact between the chamber-dividing walls (septa) and the outer shell.

### 165–163 MYA: Jurassic Period
Around 23:00, Pangaea began to break apart, creating new seas where ammonites and giant marine reptiles swam. Later in the Jurassic Period, the central Atlantic Ocean started to open, separating North America from Africa.

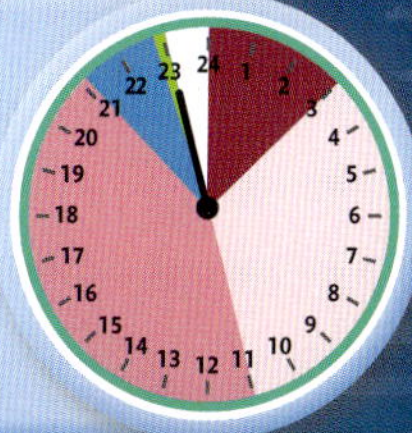

## BUOYANT BEAUTIES
Ammonites were highly mobile carnivores. They moved up and down the shallow waters by regulating the amount of gas and water in their chambers, a bit like modern submarines.

**Buoyancy control**
The hollow inner chambers acted like air tanks to help ammonites float.

### FOSSIL HUNTING
In the southwest of England is a stretch of cliffs known as the Jurassic Coast. Here, the crumbling cliffs often reveal new treasures from that period and amateur fossil hunters search for ammonites on the rocky beaches.

### HIDDEN TREASURE
Unremarkable sedimentary rock split in half can reveal fossils. Here two ammonite shells are each preserved as a hollow mould (left) in one half and a raised cast (right) in the other.

### LIVING RELATIVE
Today, the nautilus, a mollusc with an elegant patterned shell, helps us imagine how ammonites may have lived and moved. It lives in the deep waters of the Indo-Pacific Ocean.

|57

**125-120 MYA** CRETACEOUS PERIOD

# TAKING FLIGHT

Early Cretaceous fossils from northeast China tell stories of forests filled with primitive birds and feathered dinosaurs. Perched, gliding, flying, or running among the trees are theropods – the carnivorous ancestors of modern birds – and other bird-relatives.

### 1 Perched for success
*Yixianosaurus* uses its long arms to reach tall branches and grasp tasty seeds from a ginkgo tree. This small climber belongs to a theropod group called paravians, meaning "near birds".

### 2 Lost group
*Longipteryx*, one of the strongest flyers at this time, glides between trees. It belongs to a diverse group of birds called enantiornithines, but none of them survive to the present day.

### 3 Hands before wings
This wingless meat-eater lunges towards its prey. *Sinosauropteryx* is a maniraptor – a theropod with long-fingered arms that are destined to evolve into the first wings.

### 4 Toothless flapper
With long, showy tail feathers trailing behind it, this male *Confuciusornis* makes a lucky escape. It can use the claws on its wings to climb among the trees, and like all modern birds, it has a toothless beak.

### 5 Fluffy tyrant
Thumping through the forest is the fearsome, meat-eating theropod *Yutyrannus*. Weighing 1.3 tonnes (1.4 tons), this tyrannosaur is covered in feathers that keep it warm during chilly winters.

### 6 Three-fingered dragon
*Dilong*, which translates to "emperor dragon" in Chinese, stalks the forest floor, looking for its next meal. This small relative of a *Tyrannosaurus* has a downy coat.

### 7 Near-modern bird
Pigeon-sized *Archaeorhynchus* is enjoying a bath in a forest pool. This ancient bird with a toothless beak shares many features with modern birds.

There is evidence for simple, hair-like feathers in some tyrannosaurs.

Tyrannosaurus's bite was incredibly powerful, around three times that of a lion.

**Tyrannosaurus**
Though not a direct ancestor of birds, this fellow theropod shared their upright, two-legged posture and hollow bones.

**Velociraptor**
This Late Cretaceous theropod had evolved long feathered arms, but it could not fly.

Long, wing-like feathers probably evolved for display.

**TAKING FLIGHT**
Before *Tyrannosaurus* ruled the land, bird ancestors were already developing. Some had feathers, wings, claws, and sharp teeth, and may have glided between trees. Over time, they evolved the muscles and bones for powered flight.

# EVOLUTION OF BIRDS

It might not seem like *Tyrannosaurus rex* has much in common with a pigeon, but birds are living dinosaurs that evolved from small, feathered theropods. Fossils found in China revealed a stunning array of feathered dinosaurs, suggesting that feathers evolved for warmth and display before they were adapted for flight.

**125–120 mya: Jurassic Period**
Around 23:20, Earth was warm and largely ice-free. Forests full of early birds and other dinosaurs flourished on land, from the equator to the poles. Sea levels were up to 170 m (558 ft) higher than today.

**Archaeopteryx**
This bird ancestor combined bird-like features, such as large feathers and a wishbone, with reptilian ones such as teeth, a bony tail, and clawed fingers.

**Pigeon**
Modern birds evolved after the extinction of all non-bird dinosaurs, becoming lighter, more efficient flyers.

Modern bird wings are adapted for strong, sustained flight.

Claws on its wings may have helped *Archaeopteryx* climb trees or hold prey.

Early birds had long, bony tails, much like non-flying dinosaurs.

**Keel**
This big ridge of bone anchors the powerful muscles birds need to fly.

**Feathers**
*Archaeopteryx* had flat feathers with a central quill, similar to modern birds.

### ARCHAEOPTERYX
Fossils of this Late Jurassic, magpie-sized dinosaur preserve feathers, soft tissues, and tiny bones, helping palaeontologists understand how birds have evolved

### HOLLOW BONES
Bird bones are full of cavities. Hollow, air-filled bones help make birds light and agile, but they evolved in some dinosaurs about 240 mya, long before the first birds.

c.113 MYA  CRETACEOUS PERIOD

# THE ARRIVAL OF FLOWERS

Near the tranquil waters of a Cretaceous lagoon, beetles buzz from flower to flower, and ancient wasps and mayflies fill the air. The first flowers have evolved, and with them the first pollinators. Amid the conifers and ferns, brand new shapes and colours burst into bloom.

**1 Hovering mayfly**
This insect has spent most of its life as a larva in the waters of the lagoon, before emerging to reproduce. Mayflies are among the first winged insects to evolve.

**2 Unfurling fern**
This small fern, called *Ruffordia*, uses spores to reproduce, as ferns still do today, rather than growing flowers and seeds. Strong tissues help it grow tall.

**3 Flowering plants**
Water lilies, an early group of flowering plants, float in the lagoon. Flowering plants are called angiosperms, meaning "enclosed seeds", as the seeds are nestled inside the fruit, which forms after flowering.

**4 Ancient magnolia**
The first flowers to evolve are similar to modern magnolias. While dinosaurs and other plant-eaters feast on shoots and leaves, it's the energy-dense pollen that attracts pollinating insects.

**5 Hell ant attack**
This cricket is under attack from hell ants, an ancient group of ants with horns and powerful, scythe-like jaws. These sophisticated predators can hunt down insects much larger than themselves.

**6 Smelly ginkgo seeds**
This gymnosperm, a flowerless plant whose seeds are not enclosed within a fruit, uses wind to disperse pollen. Soon, angiosperms will replace gymnosperms as the dominant plants in many areas.

**7 Soft landing**
This tumbling flower beetle feasts on pollen inside an early flower. As it feeds, some pollen will stick to it and later be carried to other flowers.

**c.113 MYA: Cretaceous Period**
At 23:20 Pangaea continued to split into smaller pieces of land. North America was divided into two landmasses by an enormous sea that was up to 760 m (half a mile) deep.

## ALL ABUZZ
Today flowering plants use different pollination methods. Some rely on wind, others on animals – including insects, birds, and bats. The earliest prehistoric magnolias probably relied on beetles.

# EARLY POLLINATORS

Until the Early Cretaceous Period, plants reproduced using spores or seeds grown inside cones. Then some plants began to produce their seeds from flowers – and came to rely on insects to pollinate these. Insects were rewarded for their help with meals of pollen or nectar, and this two-way relationship, known as co-evolution, spread around the world.

## TRAPPED IN AMBER
Amber, the fossilized resin produced by some trees when they are damaged, can contain evidence of prehistoric pollination – such as insects trapped with pollen grains that they carried from plant to plant.

**Pollen meal**
This beetle used its specialized mouthparts to chew on pollen.

**Reproductive organs**
Each flower contained both male and female parts. This male part is the stamen.

**Tumbling flower beetle**
These beetles used stocky hind legs to hop or tumble around vegetation.

**c.66 MYA** CRETACEOUS PERIOD

# A DINOSAUR'S WORLD

In what is now the Hell Creek Formation of North America – a site famous for its rich fossil finds – brackish swamps give way to an inland sea. The warm, humid air of the Cretaceous Period fills the lungs of a diverse range of incredible dinosaurs as they roam the land in search of food.

**1 Subtropical forest**
In the woodlands, flowering plants co-exist with conifers. The cover of vegetation helps early mammals and other small creatures hide from larger predators.

**2 Edmontosaurus**
This duck-billed herbivore grazes on shrubs, helping to keep the forest in check. Having just spotted a *Tyrannosaurus* nearby, the dinosaur is about to run back to its herd.

**3 Crested oviraptor**
This small oviraptor, *Anzu wyliei*, shows off its colourful, broad head crest as a means of attracting potential mates. An early cousin of flying birds, it walks upright on two legs, and has feathery arms and tail.

**4 Thescelosaurus**
Making use of its strong shoulders and arms, this herbivore starts burrowing into the ground in an attempt to hide from nearby carnivores.

**5 Tyrannosaurus rex**
Up to 12 m (40 ft) long, this fearsome carnivore is used to hunting elephant-sized prey. Having waited for the perfect moment to strike, the *Tyrannosaurus* launches its attack on the *Ankylosaurus*.

**6 Ankylosaurus**
This dinosaur is 8 m (26 ft) long and has extensive body armour and a large club at the end of its tail to help it withstand the *Tyrannosaurus*'s ambush.

**7 Triceratops battle**
Using their menacing horns, two rivals weighing 10 tonnes (11 tons) each engage in head-to-head combat. Hot steam rises from their nostrils as they battle it out for dominance.

# DINOSAURS THROUGH TIME

Life recovered slowly after the Permian mass extinction. Reptiles ruled, but dinosaurs did not evolve until around 240 mya. During the Jurassic and Cretaceous periods, dinosaurs dominated the land – scientists estimate there were at least 2,000 different species.

## A MATTER OF POSTURE
Many early reptiles sprawled with legs either side of their low-slung bodies, but dinosaurs evolved fully upright hind legs that could support larger, heavier bodies. Crocodile relatives could sprawl when resting or walk semi-upright.

**Sprawling limbs**
The limbs stick out to the sides, keeping the body low to the ground, like a lizard's.

**High walk**
Crocodile relatives' limbs were partly to the side, but the body was lifted up while walking.

**Straight legs**
Dinosaur legs sat directly under the body to support the animal's weight, just like in modern mammals.

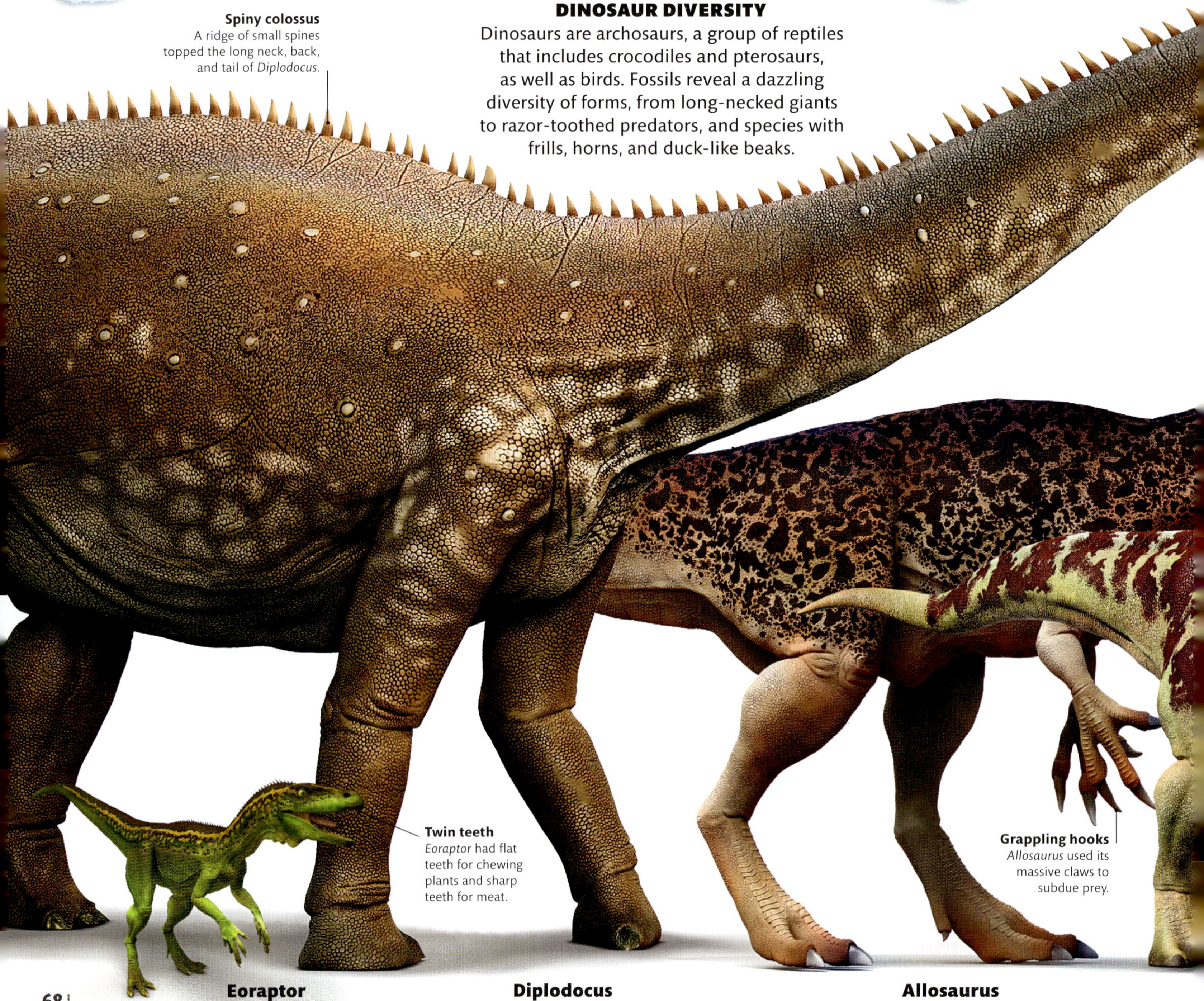

**Spiny colossus**
A ridge of small spines topped the long neck, back, and tail of *Diplodocus*.

## DINOSAUR DIVERSITY
Dinosaurs are archosaurs, a group of reptiles that includes crocodiles and pterosaurs, as well as birds. Fossils reveal a dazzling diversity of forms, from long-necked giants to razor-toothed predators, and species with frills, horns, and duck-like beaks.

**Twin teeth**
*Eoraptor* had flat teeth for chewing plants and sharp teeth for meat.

**Grappling hooks**
*Allosaurus* used its massive claws to subdue prey.

**Eoraptor**
1.7 m (5.5 ft) long, 228 mya

**Diplodocus**
33 m (108 ft) long, 150 mya

**Allosaurus**
12 m (39 ft) long, 150 mya

## NIGHT SHIFT
Alongside the dinosaurs, another group emerged. Early mammals were small, furry, shrew-like creatures and most active at night. Despite reptiles' dominance, many mammal species evolved, including climbers, diggers, gliders, and swimmers.

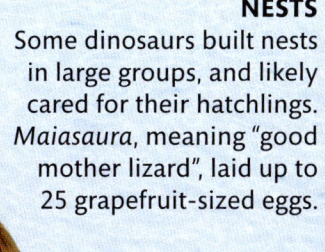

**Megazostrodon**
This tiny mammal lived 200 MYA.

## NESTS
Some dinosaurs built nests in large groups, and likely cared for their hatchlings. *Maiasaura*, meaning "good mother lizard", laid up to 25 grapefruit-sized eggs.

| TRIASSIC (252–201 MYA) | JURASSIC (201–145 MYA) | CRETACEOUS (145–66 MYA) |
|---|---|---|
| **Dinosaur family tree** Nearly 1,000 dinosaur species have been found so far and scientists are still trying to piece together how they evolved. | Sauropods *Diplodocus* | Sauropods *Argentinosaurus* |
| Saurischians *Eoraptor* | Theropods *Allosaurus* | Theropods *Velociraptor* |
| Early dinosaurs *Herrerasaurus* | Marginocephalians *Chaoyangsaurus* | Marginocephalians *Pachycephalosaurus* |
| Ornithischians *Heterodontosaurus* | Thyreophorans *Stegosaurus* | Thyreophorans *Euoplocephalus* |

**Leafy grinder**
This beaked herbivore used its curved, grooved teeth to chew plants.

**235–66 MYA: Mesozoic Era**
Between 22:45 and 23:38, dinosaurs ruled the land. In the seas, underwater volcanoes spewed out gases, causing marine life to perish. The Indian plate started to move north towards Asia.

**Curved claws**
This feathered carnivore had three long, curved claws on each of its hands.

**Iguanodon**
9 m (29.5 ft) long, 130 MYA

**Struthiomimus**
4.3 m (14 ft) long, 77 MYA

**Euoplocephalus**
7 m (23 ft) long, 70 MYA

**c.66 MYA** END CRETACEOUS PERIOD

# ASTEROID IMPACT

Life changes forever as a space rock bigger than Mount Everest smashes into Earth. An intense blast of heat scorches the ground and ash blocks out the Sun. A mass extinction ensues and ends the Cretaceous Period. About 75 per cent of all species die out, including all dinosaurs except birds.

**① Apocalyptic impact**
An asteroid 10–15 km (6–9 miles) wide crashes into shallow water off today's Yucatán Peninsula in Mexico, blasting a crater 180 km (112 miles) wide.

**② Final flight**
Pterosaur *Quetzalcoatlus* battles scalding winds. The largest animal ever to take flight, with a wingspan of up to 12 m (40 ft), will soon disappear from the skies.

**③ Giant waves**
A mega-tsunami triggered by the impact throws up waves 1.5 km (0.9 miles) high. It washes 100 km (62 miles) into North America, churns up the Atlantic seafloor, and sends waves around the world's oceans.

**④ Rain of fire**
Molten rock, launched into space by the asteroid impact, rains down all over Earth. The heat is so intense that small mammals that can shelter underground have more chance of survival.

**⑤ Crested herbivores**
Duck-billed dinosaurs called hadrosaurs call out, using their head crests to amplify the sound, but the roar of destruction drowns them out.

**⑥ Horned dinosaur escape**
*Coahuilaceratops*, a large herbivore related to *Triceratops*, attempts to escape. At 1.2 m (4 ft) long, its horns are some of the largest among dinosaurs.

**⑦ Spring bloom**
Magnolias are in bloom, suggesting it is spring in the northern hemisphere when the asteroid strikes. Following the impact, it is ferns rather than flowering plants that recover first.

**⑧ Terrified tyrant**
Theropod *Labocania*, a fearsome ambush hunter, perishes at this time. As top predators die out, other groups, such as mammals, will thrive.

## ASTEROID IMPACT

In 1980, two scientists found evidence that a giant asteroid, a space rock orbiting the Sun, struck Earth 66 MYA. Since then, other scientists have found more and more signs of a devastating impact.

The asteroid hurtled towards Earth at about 20 km/s (12 mps).

**1 Shocking impact**
The rock crashed to Earth with more force than all the nuclear weapons ever made.

A quartz grain near the impact site has been "shocked", resulting in many parallel lines.

Ash and dust from eruptions circled the globe and blocked out the Sun, causing initial cooling.

The ash and dust finally settled, but greenhouse gases from the eruption lasted for far longer, causing long-term global warming.

Runny lava spread over an area of 500,000 sq km (200,000 sq miles), forming a layer of basalt 2 km (1.3 miles) thick. Today, these hills are called the Deccan Traps.

## VOLCANIC ACTIVITY

The natural world was already under stress when the asteroid struck. India had begun passing over a volcanic "hotspot", which caused massive, irregular surges in volcanic activity for 2 million years. This made Earth's climate unstable and our planet a difficult place to survive.

The asteroid struck at an angle of between 45° and 60°.

A thin layer of iridium has been found in rocks dating back to 66 MYA all around the world. This element is far more common in asteroids than in Earth's crust.

**3 Ash cloud**
The asteroid vaporized on impact, hurling dust and ash into the atmosphere. This ash cloud blotted out the Sun, plunging Earth into darkness for a year or more, before settling.

**2 Shockwaves**
The impact caused a massive tsunami, but also sent shockwaves through the Earth. These caused violent waves in narrow waterways around the world. At Hell Creek, USA, palaeontologists have found piles of fossilized fish that were hurled ashore by these waves.

**66 MYA: Cretaceous Period**
The oceans around the world were widening, and the southern Atlantic Ocean had opened. Australia and Antarctica were still joined together. Around 23:38, a massive asteroid hit Earth.

# DOUBLE DISASTER

How can we tell what caused the mass extinction 66 MYA and wiped out all giant dinosaurs? Piecing together the evidence has taken years of research by Earth scientists, but two main theories have emerged – a devastating asteroid impact and massive volcanic activity. It is likely that both contributed to the catastrophe.

**IMPACT SITE**
By chance, researchers discovered a crater 180 km (112 miles) wide in modern-day Mexico's Yucatán Peninsula, buried under 1 km (0.6 miles) of sediment. This find was clear proof of a massive asteroid impact.

**SURVIVORS**
As the dust settled around the world, small quail-like birds, turtles, snakes, crocodiles, and mammals were among the animals to emerge from the destruction. With many of their predators and competitors gone, they evolved to colonize new habitats.

73

# THE AGE OF MAMMALS

**Woolly mammoth**
During the last ice age, herds of woolly mammoths lived in grasslands that bordered the ice sheets of the northern continents. These magnificent creatures were well adapted to life in the cold.

**c.55–20 MYA** EOCENE TO MIOCENE EPOCHS

# CONTINENTS COLLIDE

An enormous collision occurs between the Indian and Eurasian plates, crumpling and thickening Earth's crust into mountains that will become the tallest on Earth, the Himalayas. After the collision of the continents, animals of Eurasian origin mix with those from India and coexist in the warm, humid forests and foothills.

**1 Snowy peaks**
The Himalayas are still rising as the Indian plate pushes into Eurasia, a movement that continues today. Snow covers the mountain tops, occasionally tumbling down in avalanches, while the lower slopes are covered in conifer-rich woodlands.

**2 Large-scale folds**
When mountains form as a result of two continents colliding, the rocks in between are squashed and heated by the pressure. This causes the layers of rock to fold and buckle, forming intricate striped patterns on the mountainsides.

**3 Gliding lizard**
Small animals of Asian origin, such as Draco lizards, begin to glide from tree to tree. Dipterocarps – tall trees with few branches on the lower parts of their trunks – create the ideal conditions for gliding.

**4 Pig-sized mammals**
Grazing the foothills are the hoofed mammals *Cambaytherium*. With an odd number of toes on their hind feet, these ancestors of rhinos, horses, and tapirs are thought to have evolved in India when it was still an island.

**5 Floodplain**
Long, meandering rivers including the Ganges and Indus flow down from the Himalayas, carrying sediments and depositing them in vast plains. This makes the ground at the foot of the mountains fertile.

**6 Rabbit-sized sprinter**
*Diacodexis*'s relatively long legs are adapted for bursts of movement. Of Asian origin, these small, long-tailed herbivores are the earliest known artiodactyls, a group of even-toed, hoofed mammals that later includes deer, hippos, and camels.

# MAKING MOUNTAINS

Mountains have formed in a wide variety of dramatic ways over Earth's turbulent history. The Himalayas, the world's tallest mountains today, formed when two tectonic plates, the Indian and Eurasian plates, collided and crumpled up.

## COLLISION COURSE

The formation of the Himalayas took place over millions of years. Its story began when supercontinent Pangaea started to break apart 180 million years ago and India started drifting north, on a collision course with Asia.

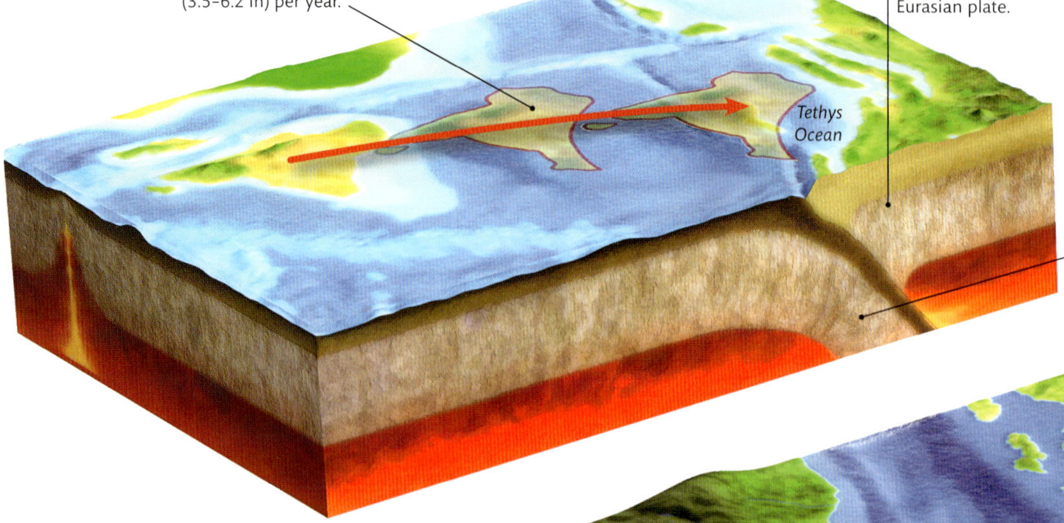

India was moving north at a rate of 9–16 cm (3.5–6.2 in) per year.

Asia sits on the thick continental crust of the Eurasian plate.

Tethys Ocean

Ocean crust sinks below continental crust.

In Asia, a chain of volcanoes formed where magma erupted as lava.

**① Passage north**
Around 80 MYA, India lay 6,400 km (4,000 miles) south of Asia. As India moved north, the Tethys Ocean, located between India and Asia, slowly closed up.

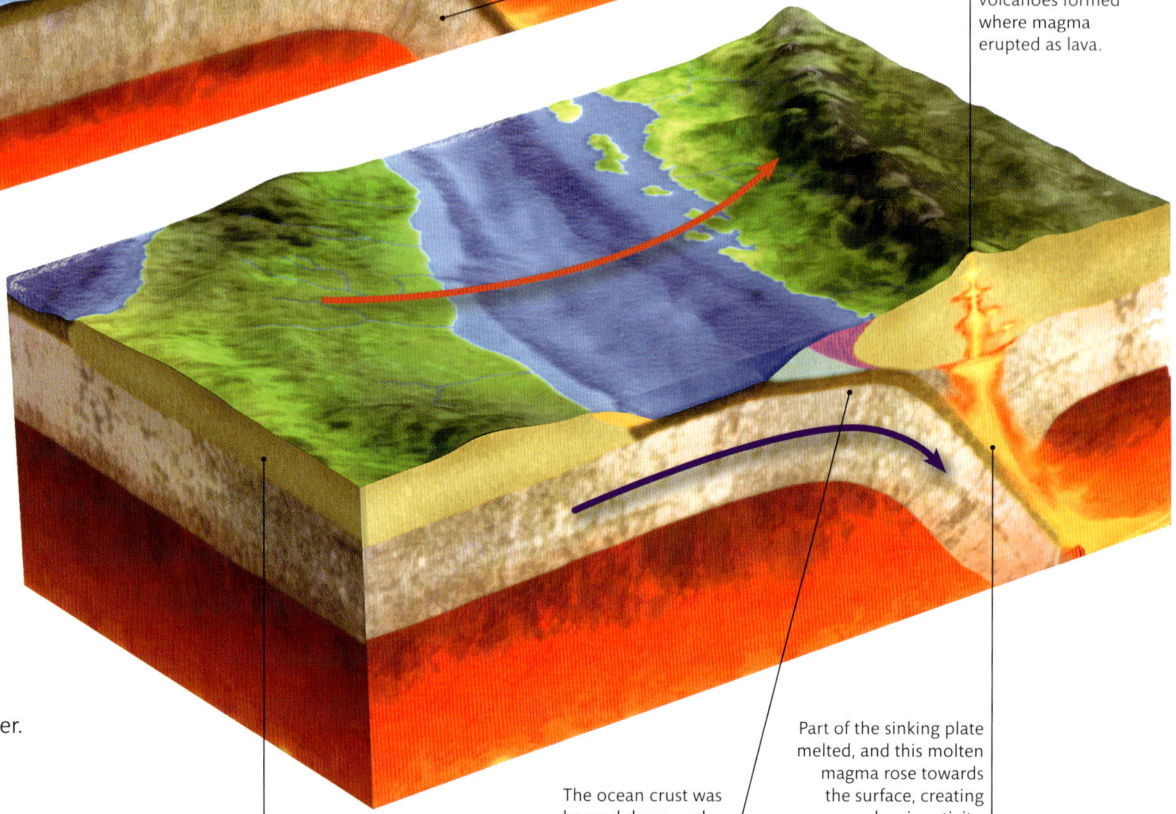

**② Narrow basin**
As the denser ocean crust between India and Asia was dragged under the lighter Eurasian plate, the ocean became narrower and narrower.

By this time, India's northward drift had slowed to around 4–6 cm (1.6–2.4 in) per year.

The ocean crust was dragged down under the continental crust, taking water with it.

Part of the sinking plate melted, and this molten magma rose towards the surface, creating volcanic activity.

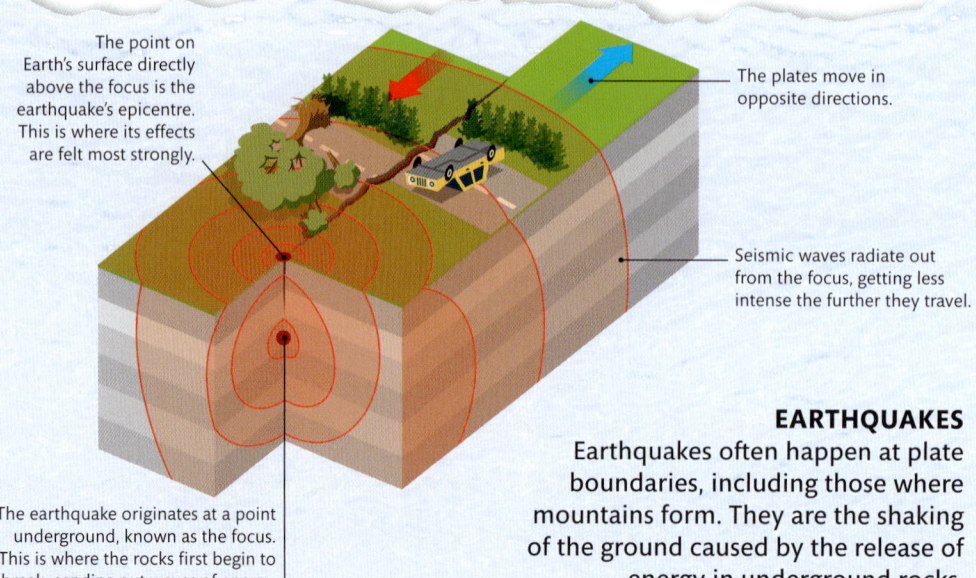

The point on Earth's surface directly above the focus is the earthquake's epicentre. This is where its effects are felt most strongly.

The plates move in opposite directions.

Seismic waves radiate out from the focus, getting less intense the further they travel.

The earthquake originates at a point underground, known as the focus. This is where the rocks first begin to break, sending out waves of energy.

## EARTHQUAKES

Earthquakes often happen at plate boundaries, including those where mountains form. They are the shaking of the ground caused by the release of energy in underground rocks.

## TYPES OF MOUNTAIN

Most mountains form when two tectonic plates collide, or when magma pushes Earth's crust up. Others form when mounds of lava from volcanoes accumulate over time, or due to folding and faulting.

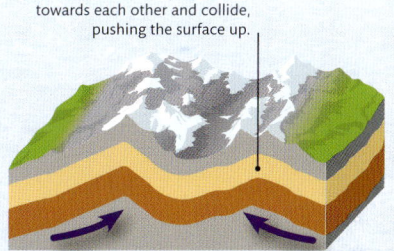

Continental plates move towards each other and collide, pushing the surface up.

**Fold mountains**
Most of Earth's mountains, including the Himalayas, formed when rock layers in the crust became folded and crumpled, and rose up. Folds may be visible on a mountainside millions of years later.

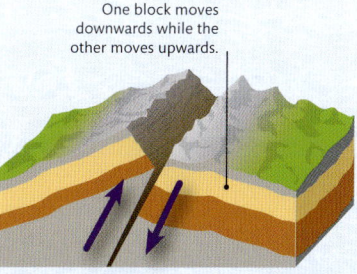

One block moves downwards while the other moves upwards.

**Fault block mountains**
Rock may crack, or "fault", under pressure, breaking into blocks. When the crust is stretched and thinned, one block may be pushed up and the other down, forming steep mountains and valleys.

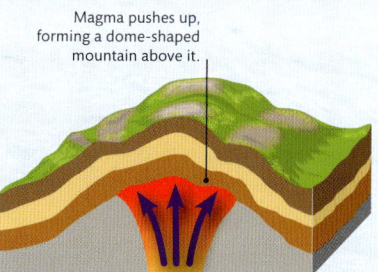

Magma pushes up, forming a dome-shaped mountain above it.

**Dome mountains**
When magma rising through Earth's mantle pushes up Earth's crust, the surface bulges upwards, forming dome-shaped mountains. The magma beneath cools and solidifies into a type of igneous rock.

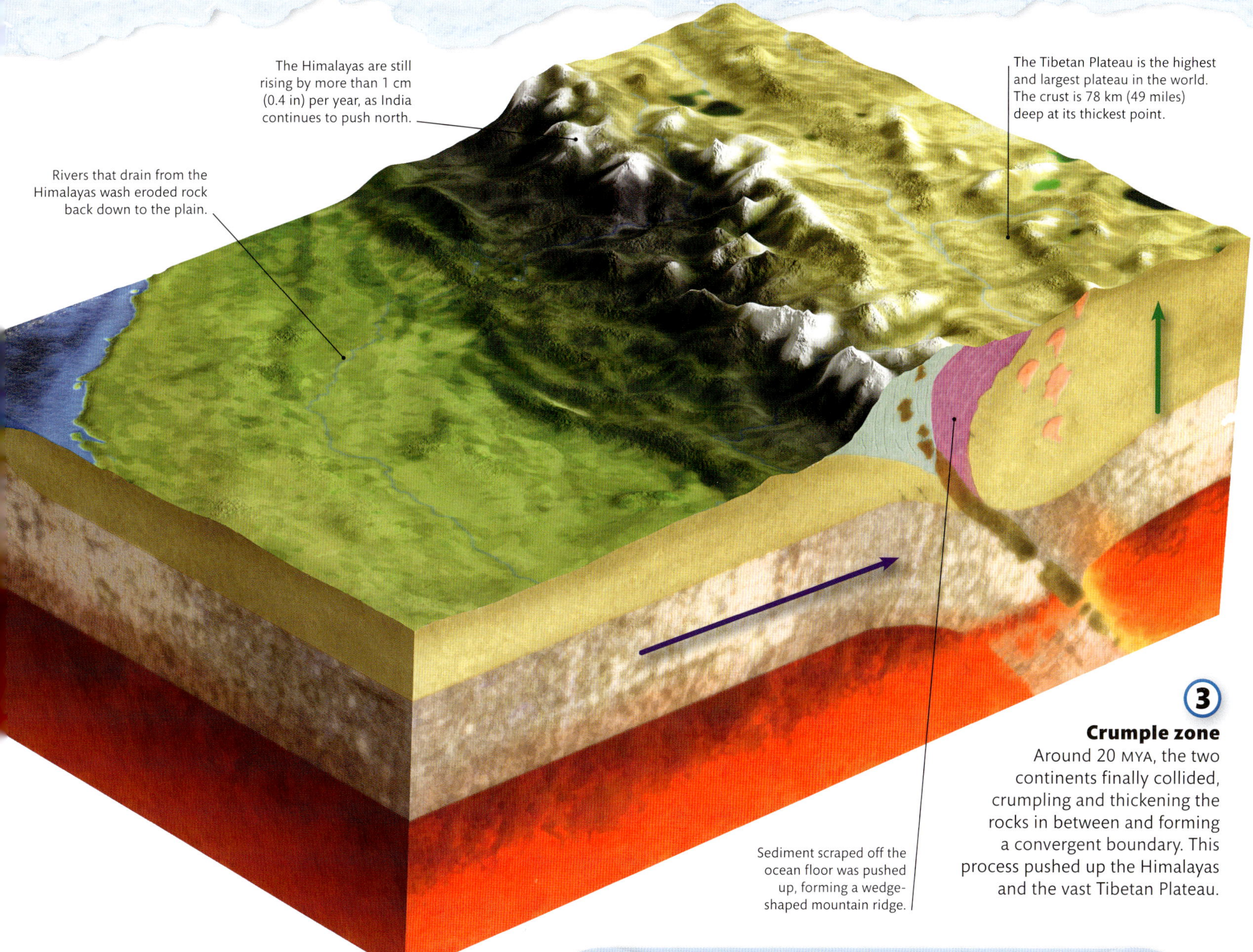

---

The Himalayas are still rising by more than 1 cm (0.4 in) per year, as India continues to push north.

The Tibetan Plateau is the highest and largest plateau in the world. The crust is 78 km (49 miles) deep at its thickest point.

Rivers that drain from the Himalayas wash eroded rock back down to the plain.

Sediment scraped off the ocean floor was pushed up, forming a wedge-shaped mountain ridge.

### ③ Crumple zone
Around 20 MYA, the two continents finally collided, crumpling and thickening the rocks in between and forming a convergent boundary. This process pushed up the Himalayas and the vast Tibetan Plateau.

**c.55–20 MYA: Eocene to Miocene Epochs**
Around 23:45, India began its multimillion-year collision with Asia. Also at this time, Australia separated from Antarctica and started to move north.

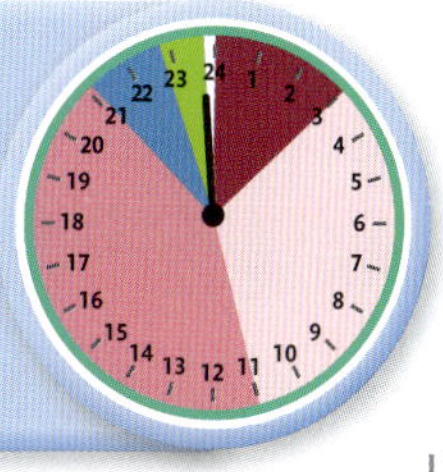

79

**c.41–39 MYA** EOCENE EPOCH

# TROPICAL FORESTS

In the Eocene Epoch, a lush, colourful forest covers this area of South America. From the lower slopes of the Andes mountains all the way to the sea, a rich variety of mammals and birds live among the cashews, palms, woody vines, and mangroves. Nearby waters are home to penguins and crocodiles.

**1 Warm forest**
This dense forest is growing in a much warmer climate than today. During the Early Eocene, global average temperatures reached a balmy 27°C (81°F), almost double today's average.

**2 Squirrel-sized monkeys**
Two *Perupithecus* monkeys are preening under the leaves of tall *Cariniana* trees. Trees that grow high above the rest of the forest are called emergents.

**3 Chinchilla relative**
Amid the dense canopy, mouse-sized rodents nibble on seeds, fruit, and leaves. They are thought to have evolved in Africa, before crossing to South America.

**4 Lurking reptile**
A crocodile, lurking among the thick roots of *Avicennia* mangrove trees, waits to ambush its next meal – perhaps an unwary rodent.

**5 Kapok ancestor**
These lofty canopy trees are the ancestors of modern kapok trees. Palaeontologists know a great deal about these ancient forests thanks to preserved fossil trees, formed when volcanic eruptions swept up logs and buried them.

**6 Terrifying attack**
A young caviomorph has fallen victim to this fearsome predator. The aptly named terror bird stands up to 2 m (6.5 ft) tall, with powerful legs and a lethal hooked beak to catch its prey.

**7 Giant penguin**
This *Inkayacu* penguin uses streamlined flippers to dive and swim in the tropical waters. Weighing 54–59 kg (119–130 lb), it is twice as heavy as a modern-day emperor penguin.

# TROPICS TRANSFORM

Today's tropical rainforests are some of Earth's richest, most diverse ecosystems. Descended from Palaeogene forests, these warm, moist habitats are home to an incredible array of organisms living among dense trees. But before the asteroid impact 66 MYA, forests looked very different.

**SELF-SUSTAINING BIOME**
Tropical rainforests such as the Amazon are self-sustaining ecosystems. They generate their own rainfall, as water evaporates into clouds and condenses as rain, while fungi recycle nutrients from plants and animals.

**CROSSING THE ATLANTIC**
Monkeys first appeared in South America 40 MYA, when it was an isolated continent. They likely floated from Africa on natural rafts of earth and vegetation, across an Atlantic Ocean that was narrower than it is today.

**CRETACEOUS FOREST**
Before the catastrophic impact that ended the Cretaceous, a light cover of conifers, flowering plants, and ferns created an open landscape. Dinosaurs would have fed on larger plants and trampled smaller shrubs, limiting their spread.

Tall conifers called monkey puzzle trees, or *Araucaria*, were widely spaced.

Conifer trees dominated the canopy, providing food for herbivores.

A fan-shaped cluster of leaves sat on the crown of *Sabalites* palms.

Seed plants such as cycads decorated the forest floor.

Dappled sunlight reached the forest floor through divided leaves of palms.

Flowering plants such as this magnolia had already evolved.

Shrubs within the laurel family and ferns made up the ground cover.

c.34 MYA EOCENE TO OLIGOCENE EPOCHS

# FREEZING WORLD

As the Eocene Epoch gives way to the Oligocene, Antarctica experiences a dramatic swing from mild temperatures and warm, wet conditions to a much colder and drier climate. On the rocky beaches at the edge of the ice sheets, one animal stands out – *Palaeeudyptes*, a mega-penguin standing 2 m (7 ft) tall.

### 1 Seymour (Marambio) Island
The shores and shallow seas of this tiny island off the coast of Antarctica teem with birds and fish. Fossils and rocks will preserve a rich record of life in Antarctica for 34 million years.

### 2 Huge hunters
With a mighty wingspan of 6 m (20 ft), *Pelagornithids* glide over the ocean like modern-day albatrosses. Sharp, tooth-like bony spikes grow out from their jawbones, ideal for seizing slippery squid and fish.

### 3 Advancing ice
The amount of carbon dioxide in Earth's air is falling, making the climate cooler. On top of this, the giant landmass of Gondwana is breaking up, so that a cold, windswept ocean forms around Antarctica. This will isolate it from warmer waters.

### 4 Beech woodland
Forests, once lush and widespread across the island, are now restricted to parts of the coast. Less hardy species have died out, so the remaining woodland is dominated by *Nothofagus*, southern beech trees.

### 5 Hungry mouths
The rocky beaches of Seymour (Marambio) Island are home to colonies of *Palaeeudyptes* penguins. Until the young birds are able to swim, parents may take it in turns to hunt for fish in the sea, returning with a meal for their growing chicks.

### 6 Going fishing
Life thrives in the cooling seas around Seymour (Marambio) Island. Small fish are an important source of food for fishing birds, as well as sand tiger sharks and *Llanocetus*, a toothed whale.

# SUPER-SIZED PENGUINS

The mega-penguin *Palaeeudyptes* would have been a giant on Antarctic beaches 34 MYA. Penguins are thought to have evolved from diving seabirds, losing their ability to fly as their wings became flippers. This enabled them to become much bigger and dive deep for plentiful fish in the waters around Seymour Island (also known as Marambio Island).

**Colossal penguin**
Although a complete mega-penguin skeleton has never been found, palaeontologists can estimate its enormous size from fossil bones.

**BEECH FORESTS**
Before the climate began to cool at the end of the Eocene, wet rainforests were dominated by *Nothofagus*, southern beech trees. These forests were lost with global cooling. They are now restricted to milder, coastal climates.

**MAMMAL BROWSERS**
The beech forests were home to Antarctic mammals such as the ungulate *Notiolofos*. Roughly the size of a musk ox, these herbivores fed on vegetation in the lush forests that stretched from South America to Antarctica.

**Palaeeudyptes**
2 m (6.6 ft)

**34 MYA: Eocene Epoch**
At 23:50, following a 20-million-year warm period, Earth froze up. After the break-up of Gondwana, a cold circumpolar current began flowing from west to east around Antarctica, allowing ice to form there.

### ANTARCTIC ISLAND
Seymour (Marambio) Island today looks very different from the tree-lined shores of the mega-penguin's time. The climate has cooled dramatically and the island has drifted south. It now features dry valleys and cliffs with some snow. Average temperatures are 1°C (33.8°F) in summer and −21°C (−5.8°F) in winter, but these are increasing due to climate change.

### Largest living penguin
The biggest of all the 18 penguin species on Earth today is the emperor. Its size, ability to maintain its body temperature, and deep diving skills for hunting fish help it survive in the freezing Antarctic waters.

**Size comparison**

### LARGER THAN LIFE
Over time, penguins have evolved to be dramatically different sizes. The mega-penguin's colossal size may have allowed it to hunt larger and deeper prey by diving for up to 40 minutes. Later, competition for food with newly evolving whales or seals drove it to extinction, while smaller penguins survived and diversified.

### HUMAN BASE
Today, humans live on the island alongside Antarctic fur seals and the Adélie penguins. Marambio Base scientific research station can be home to between 55 and 180 people at any one time, studying weather patterns and the climate.

### Compact penguin
Although the mega-penguins are long gone, more than 100,000 Adélie penguins call Seymour (Marambio) Island home. Their compact shape, a layer of fat, and dense feathers help them stay warm in Antarctica.

### World's smallest penguin
The little blue, or fairy penguin, lives in warmer New Zealand and Australia. At just over 1 kg (2.2 lb), it weighs about as much as a large pineapple.

**Emperor penguin**
1.2 m (4 ft)

**Adélie penguin**
70 cm (2.3 ft)

**Little blue penguin**
33 cm (1.1 ft)

**c.32 MYA** OLIGOCENE EPOCH

# A MAMMAL'S WORLD

In the shadow of the Andes mountains 32 MYA, Chile is home to a wide range of ancient mammals. Many are unique to South America, which is still an island at this time, isolated from other continents. These remarkable animals are about to be engulfed by devastating mudflows.

### ❶ Pocket opossum
Among the sparse trees of this cold, arid floodplain live early marsupials – mammals who carry their tiny young in the mother's pouch. These relatives of modern opossums forage for seeds in the canopy.

### ❷ Volcanoes on the rise
The Andes mountains are still rising. Their snow-capped peaks and rain-drenched slopes are active volcanoes formed as the Nazca Plate beneath the Pacific Ocean is forced under the South American Plate in a process called subduction *(see page 17)*.

### ❸ Massive mudflows
Two *Eomorphippus* – horse-like herbivores that belong to a group of mammals called notoungulates – gallop away from an incoming torrent of mud and volcanic ash. These mudflows, triggered by heavy rain, will bury and preserve these mammals as fossils.

### ❹ Bulky browser
The soft leaves of trees and shrubs attract a large ground sloth, which uses its long arms and curved claws to grasp at branches. Further away, another sloth unearths a young tree, looking for tasty morsels.

### ❺ Rhino-sized lawnmowers
*Toxodon* is a notoungulate built like a rhinoceros and nourished by rich vegetation, which is fertilized by volcanic soil. All notoungulates are destined to go extinct during the Late Pleistocene megafauna extinction, 32 million years from now.

### ❻ Chinchilla relatives
Ancient, chinchilla-like rodents, called *Eoviscaccia*, have emerged from their burrows to scan for danger. Like many of the animals nearby, they possess long, "high-crowned" teeth – teeth with thicker chewing surfaces to avoid being worn away by the rough grasses they eat.

# NEW CONNECTIONS

For millions of years, North and South America were separated by a deep ocean channel. Around 3 MYA, a piece of land called the Isthmus of Panama formed between them, allowing previously isolated animals to migrate north and south. Some spread and thrived, but others died out.

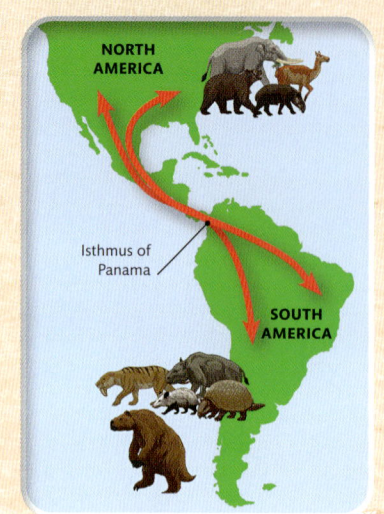

**VOLCANIC BRIDGE**
Over 150 million years, a chain of volcanoes rose between North and South America, eventually forming a chain of islands. By 3 MYA these had joined to form a land bridge – the Isthmus of Panama – and species from both sides explored strange new worlds.

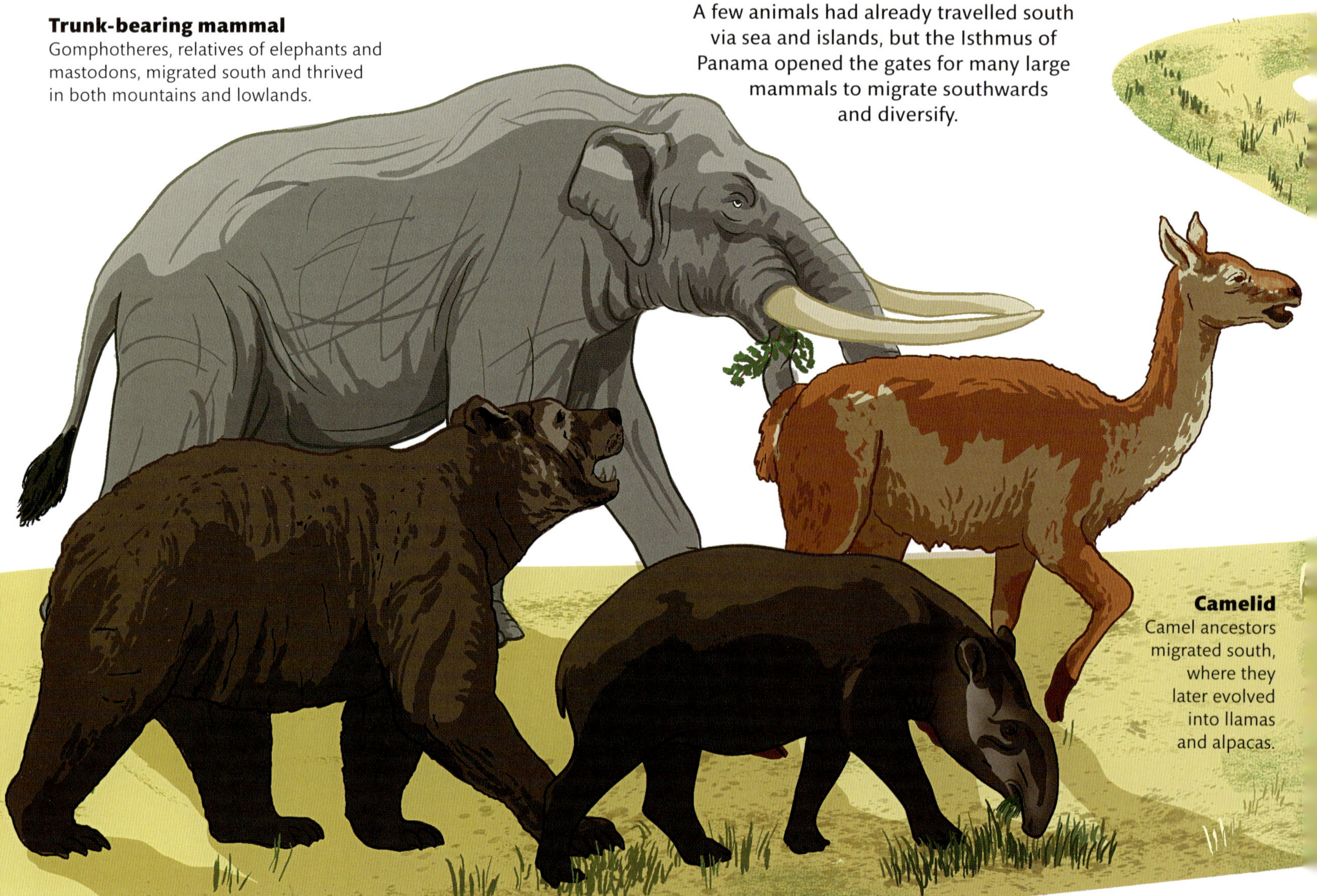

**Trunk-bearing mammal**
Gomphotheres, relatives of elephants and mastodons, migrated south and thrived in both mountains and lowlands.

**NORTH AMERICANS**
A few animals had already travelled south via sea and islands, but the Isthmus of Panama opened the gates for many large mammals to migrate southwards and diversify.

**Camelid**
Camel ancestors migrated south, where they later evolved into llamas and alpacas.

**Bear**
Short-faced bears originated in North America. Some migrated south, evolving into giant forms that are now extinct.

**Tapir**
Ancestors of this long-nosed South American mammal crossed from the north fewer than 3 MYA.

## SOUTH AMERICANS
During 30 million years of isolation, weird and wonderful species had evolved in South America. A few travelled northwards, but competition from North American rivals drove others to extinction.

**Meat-eating marsupial**
*Thylacosmilus* ("terrible pouched knife") had huge, ever-growing teeth, but died out soon after the land bridge formed.

**Toxodon**
This rhino-sized plant-eater weighed more than 1 tonne (1.1 tons). It lived on in the south until humans arrived.

**Clever marsupial**
Opossums are common in North America today, best known for playing dead when threatened.

**Glyptodon**
This heavily-armoured giant was covered in bony scales. Some settled in the southeast of North America.

**Ground sloth**
Several species of ground sloth moved north, spreading as far as modern-day Canada.

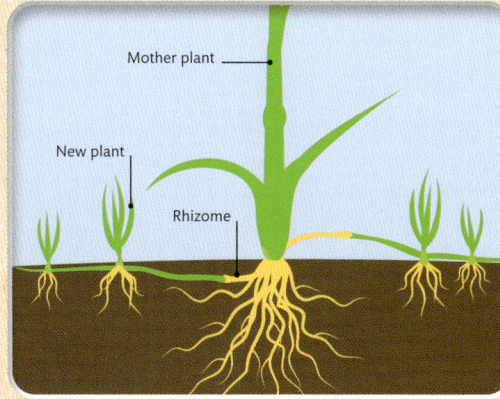

### GRAZE PERIL
During the Palaeogene, a cooling climate helped grasses spread, but with success came more grazing animals to eat them. Grass evolved ways to survive, such as by reproducing using underground shoots called rhizomes to avoid chomping teeth.

**32–3 MYA: Oligocene to Pliocene Epochs**
Between 23:50 and 23:56, mountains formed around the world. Cold grasslands spread, and grazers with them. Continents started to look more like they do today.

**c.5.3 MYA** PLIOCENE EPOCH

# MEGA FLOOD

During the Pliocene, the Mediterranean basin has mostly been dry and salty – until seawater bursts in from the Atlantic Ocean. This catastrophic event, called the Zanclean Megaflood, leaves a trail of destruction beneath the churning waves as it refills the Mediterranean, although some scientists today argue the flooding was more gradual.

**1 Atlantic gateway**
A mountain range linking Africa and Europe has been slowly sinking for centuries, until it drops below sea level and water crashes over the top. In time, this will become the Strait of Gibraltar, gateway between the Atlantic Ocean and the Mediterranean Sea.

**2 Stormy waters**
Cascading at up to 116 km/h (72 mph), as fast as a car speeding down a motorway, the floods whip up fierce winds and thunderstorms. The sheer weight of water shakes Earth's crust, causing violent earthquakes.

**3 Murderous flow**
Torrents and mudflows lasting months or years crash down the mountainside, sweeping all before them. The vast majority of organisms living in the basin die out and life will not recover for 1.7 million years.

**4 Ridges and boulders**
The teeming flood leaves grooves and ridges in the earth and dumps massive boulders on hilltops. Signs of the upheaval are still visible around the Mediterranean 5.3 million years later.

**5 Erosion channel**
Thunderous waters carve a deep channel 250 km (155 miles) long in the basin floor. The water wears away rock and sediment, and carries the debris downstream. This process of breaking up and transporting material is called erosion.

**6 Salty deposits**
Hundreds of thousands of years before the flood, the Mediterranean sea evaporated, leaving salt deposits 1.5 km (1 mile) thick. These vast salt flats will endure beneath the refilled sea for millions of years.

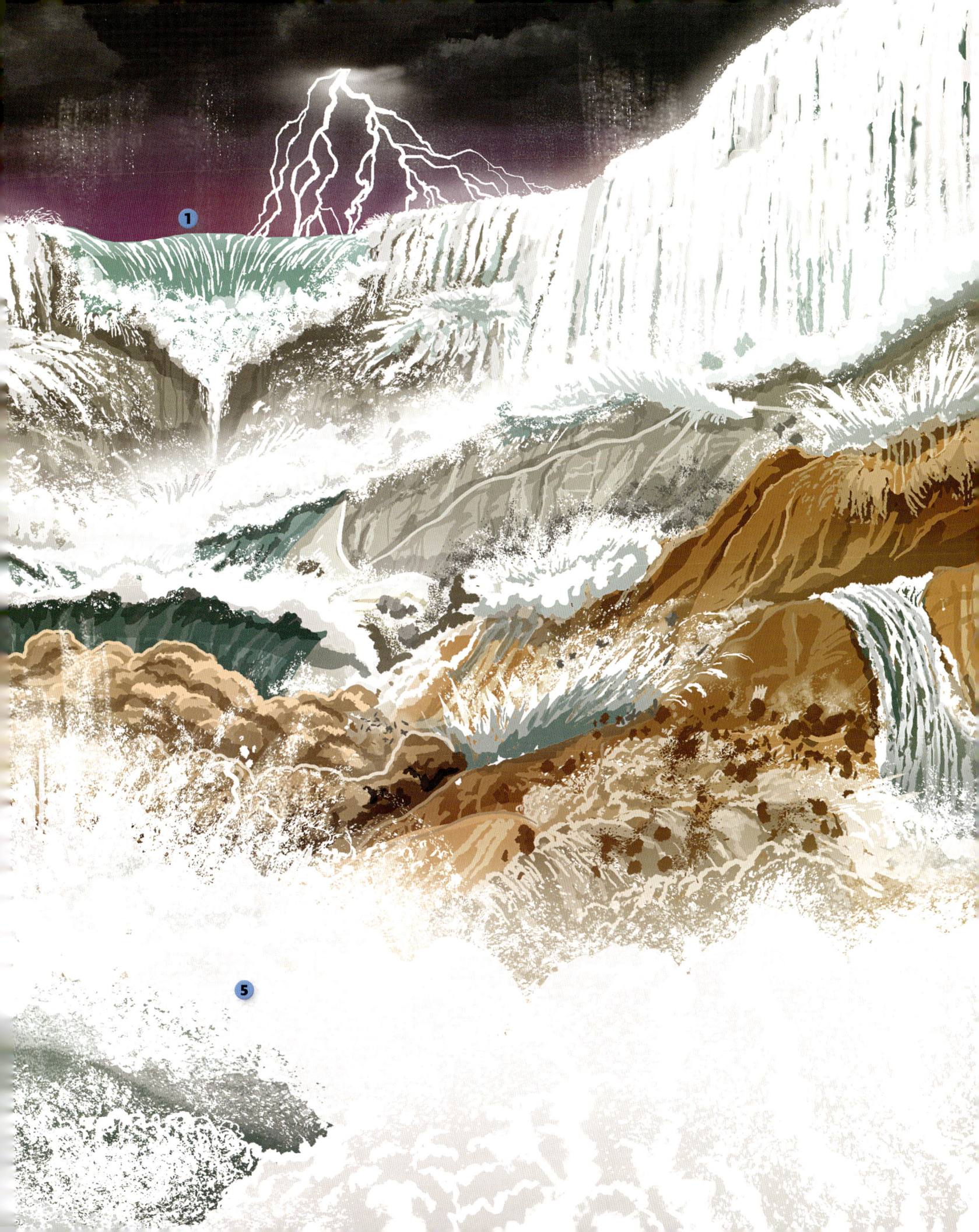

# FROM DESERT TO SEA

Before the Zanclean Megaflood, the Mediterranean basin was a desert with a few very salty lakes. When the Atlantic waters broke through *(see pages 92–93)*, they filled the western Mediterranean first. Then, as the water level rose, seawater carved a channel into the eastern Mediterranean, forming a waterfall about 1.5 km (1 mile) high.

## SEA LIFE RETURNS
In the dry period, lack of water and high salt levels in the lakes killed off most marine life in the Mediterranean. After the flood, it took more than 1.7 million years for Atlantic species such as dolphins to repopulate the sea.

## SEA SLUG INVADER
In 1869, the Suez Canal was built to link the Mediterranean Sea and the Red Sea. Invasive species moved north into the Mediterranean, including some species of sea slugs, a kind of mollusc.

## SEAS OF TIME
Scientists have used fieldwork in the Mediterranean, samples of rocks on the seabed, and computer modelling to recreate the dramatic events that they believe may have shaped the Mediterranean as we know it.

### ① Drying out
From about 8.8 to 5.3 mya, the Mediterranean was a dry basin, where the evaporation of seawater created deposits of halite (rock salt) and gypsum. The water that remained was so salty that most native sealife became extinct.

### ② Refilling
Around 5.3 mya, ocean waters rushed into the basin, filling first the west, then the east. This allowed species from the Atlantic to recolonize the Mediterranean, but sealife was slow to recover.

### ③ Sea today
The Mediterranean Sea is still saltier than most seas and continues to evaporate today, losing more than 4,000 cubic km (960 cubic miles) of water a year. However, most of this is replaced by inflow from the Atlantic Ocean.

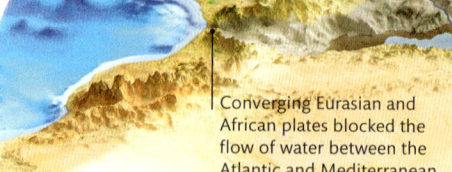

Converging Eurasian and African plates blocked the flow of water between the Atlantic and Mediterranean.

The surface of the Atlantic was hundreds of metres above the Mediterranean before it came flooding in.

The mega flood eroded a canyon through what is now the Strait of Gibraltar.

Seawater flooded the western Mediterranean, raising the sea level by more than 10 m (33 ft) a day.

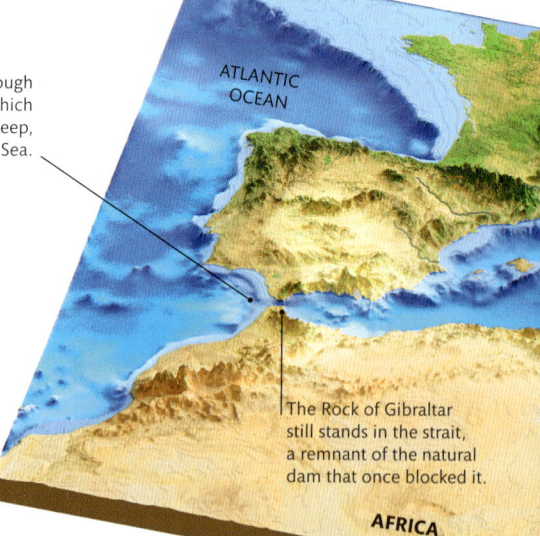

Atlantic waters flow through the Strait of Gibraltar, which is about 320 m (1,050 ft) deep, into the Mediterranean Sea.

The Rock of Gibraltar still stands in the strait, a remnant of the natural dam that once blocked it.

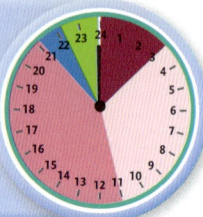

**10–4 mya: Miocene to Pliocene Epochs**
In the last five minutes, the Mediterranean Sea dried out and then refilled again. Ice grew over Antarctica, and continents reached their modern shapes and positions.

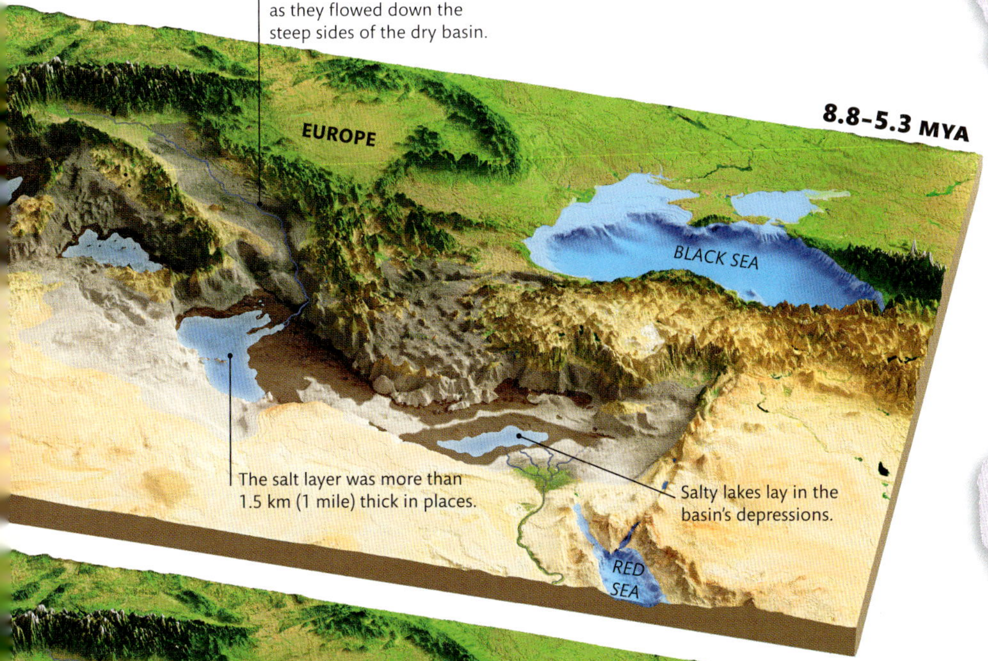

Rivers carved out ravines as they flowed down the steep sides of the dry basin.

**8.8–5.3 MYA**

EUROPE
BLACK SEA
The salt layer was more than 1.5 km (1 mile) thick in places.
Salty lakes lay in the basin's depressions.
RED SEA

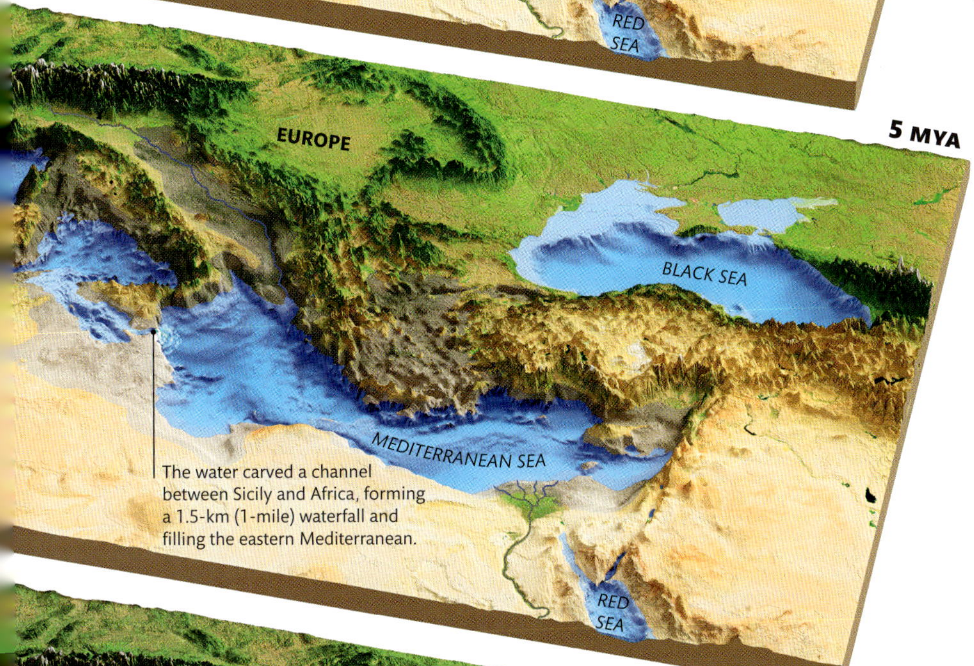

**5 MYA**

EUROPE
BLACK SEA
MEDITERRANEAN SEA
The water carved a channel between Sicily and Africa, forming a 1.5-km (1-mile) waterfall and filling the eastern Mediterranean.
RED SEA

**Present day**

EUROPE
BLACK SEA
The deepest point is more than 5 km (3 miles) deep.
MEDITERRANEAN SEA
Suez Canal
RED SEA
Sea levels continue to rise, even though the equivalent of a 1.2-m (4-ft) layer is lost from the surface every year.

## WATER POWER
Flowing water can wear down underlying rocks to form spectacular waterfalls, like the giant waterfall that formed when the Atlantic flowed into the Mediterranean during the mega flood 5.3 MYA.

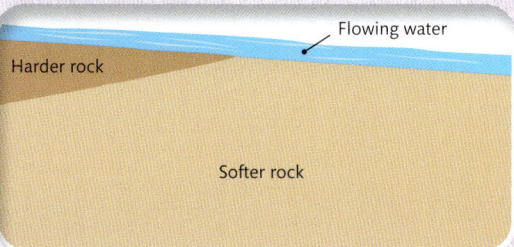

Flowing water
Harder rock
Softer rock

**1 Flowing river**
When water flows over rocks of different hardnesses, it wears away softer rock, such as sandstone or mudstone, faster than harder rock, such as granite or conglomerate.

Eroded rock particles are carried downstream.

**2 Cascading water**
As erosion of the softer rock continues, the water forms a slope. Froth, turbulence, and rock particles in the water cut the riverbed even more steeply.

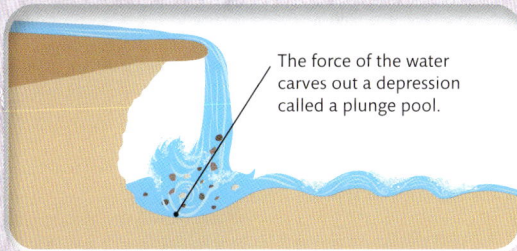

The force of the water carves out a depression called a plunge pool.

**3 Waterfall formation**
As water continues to fall and wear away the softer rock, the more resistant rock forms an overhanging ledge. The water falls into a plunge pool, which becomes deeper.

The ledge becomes unstable over time, and tumbles down.

**4 Collapse and retreat**
Over time, water will erode the harder rock too, and this will crumble into the plunge pool below, further deepening it. Slowly, erosion causes the waterfall to migrate upstream.

**c.1.8 MYA** PLEISTOCENE EPOCH

# ENTER HUMANS

In Africa's Great Rift Valley 1.8 MYA, ancestors of modern humans enter the story of evolution. In West Turkana, Kenya, a group of *Homo erectus*, which means "upright human", live on the savannah, foraging and hunting for food, and crafting tools from stone.

### 1 Sparce vegetation
In East Africa, open savannah grasslands replace woodlands from about 8 MYA to 4 MYA. With fewer trees to climb and more walking to do, moving on two legs becomes an advantage for early humans.

### 2 Water source
In the vast, arid plains herbivores and human ancestors alike meet at a watering hole – the place where all species cross paths from time to time. Most *Homo erectus* camps are found near water sources.

### 3 Large herbivores
Wildebeest, antelope, and buffalo roam the plains, occasionally serving as food for *Homo erectus*. With a mixed diet of meat and plants, early humans scavenge carcasses as well as hunting and foraging.

### 4 Upright stance
*Homo erectus* peers at wildebeest from the cover of long grass. An upright stance, with pelvis and hip bones similar to those of modern humans, allows *Homo erectus* to walk long distances.

### 5 Human proportions
*Homo erectus* has shorter arms and longer legs for its body size than its ancestors. The tall, hairless body and large brain resemble humans today, but a flatter skull, protruding brow ridge, and heavy jaw do not.

### 6 Early tools
These early humans are carving stones into hand axes and picks that will help them hunt prey and prepare food. Their tools are oval or pear-shaped, with cutting edges all the way around.

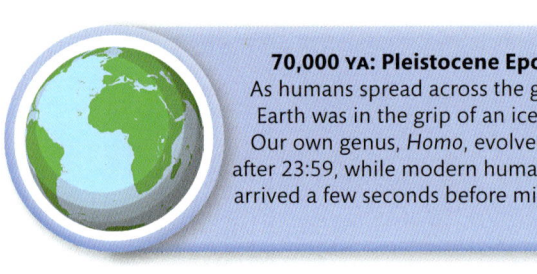

**70,000 YA: Pleistocene Epoch**
As humans spread across the globe, Earth was in the grip of an ice age. Our own genus, *Homo*, evolved just after 23:59, while modern humans only arrived a few seconds before midnight.

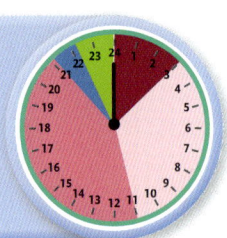

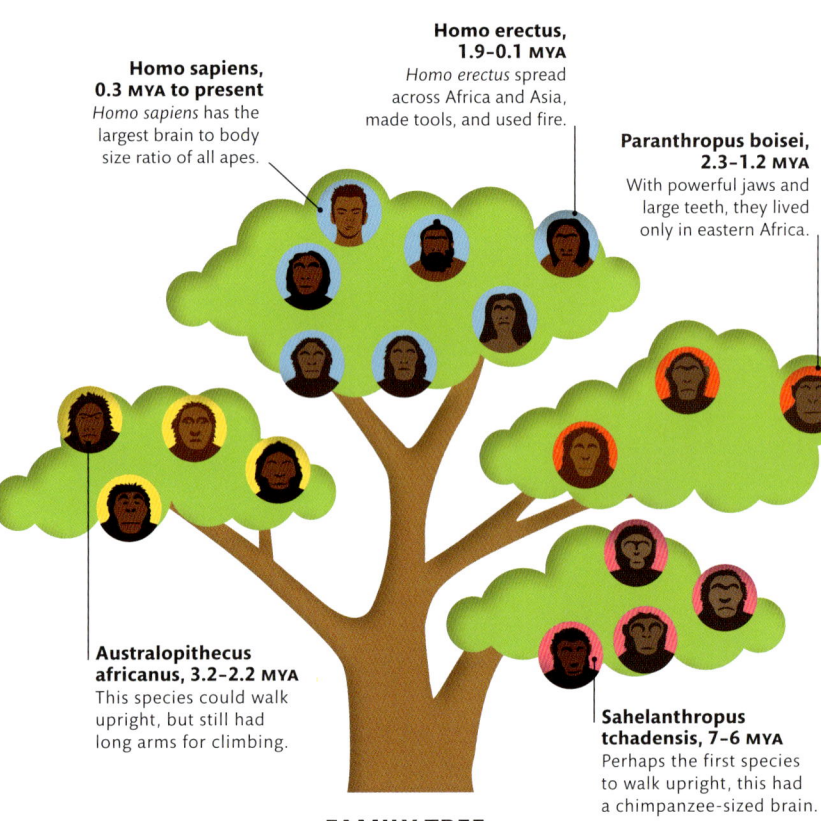

**Homo sapiens, 0.3 MYA to present**
*Homo sapiens* has the largest brain to body size ratio of all apes.

**Homo erectus, 1.9–0.1 MYA**
*Homo erectus* spread across Africa and Asia, made tools, and used fire.

**Paranthropus boisei, 2.3–1.2 MYA**
With powerful jaws and large teeth, they lived only in eastern Africa.

**Australopithecus africanus, 3.2–2.2 MYA**
This species could walk upright, but still had long arms for climbing.

**Sahelanthropus tchadensis, 7–6 MYA**
Perhaps the first species to walk upright, this had a chimpanzee-sized brain.

### FAMILY TREE
About 7 MYA, our ancestors branched off from those of our closest living relatives, chimpanzees and bonobos. Our branch, *Homo*, evolved about 2 MYA, later giving rise to *Homo sapiens*. Scientists are still researching why we are the only human species alive today.

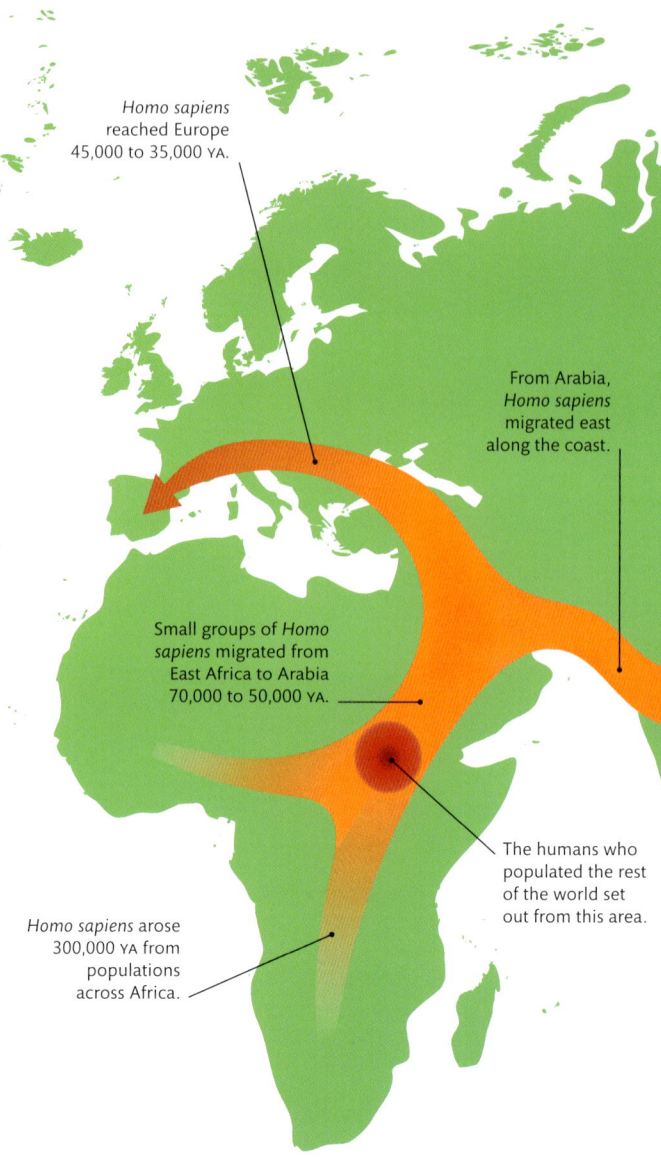

*Homo sapiens* reached Europe 45,000 to 35,000 YA.

From Arabia, *Homo sapiens* migrated east along the coast.

Small groups of *Homo sapiens* migrated from East Africa to Arabia 70,000 to 50,000 YA.

The humans who populated the rest of the world set out from this area.

*Homo sapiens* arose 300,000 YA from populations across Africa.

### CROSSING CONTINENTS
*Homo sapiens* – our species – evolved in Africa before spreading around the globe. Low sea levels and a stable climate helped humans reach and settle new lands.

# HUMAN MIGRATION

There have been more than 20 species of early human, but today only one survives. *Homo sapiens* ("wise human"), evolved across Africa 300,000 YA. Less than 70,000 YA, some of them left Africa – their descendants would go on to populate the rest of the world.

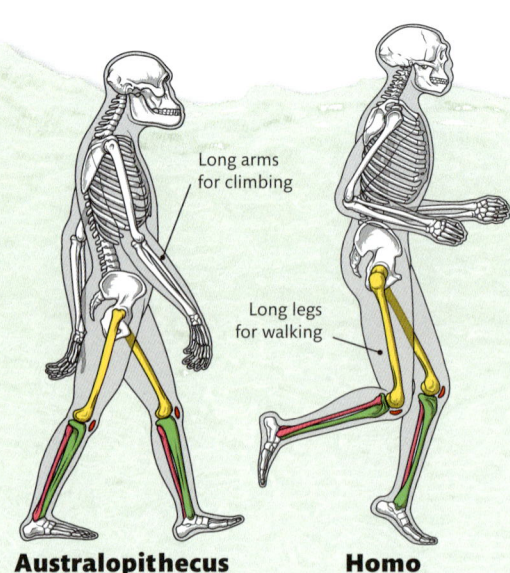

Long arms for climbing

Long legs for walking

**Australopithecus africanus**

**Homo erectus**

### WALKING TALL
Early human relatives such as *Australopithecus* could walk upright, but were still adapted for climbing too. *Homo erectus*, meaning "upright human", had longer legs and shorter arms designed for life on two legs, including walking long distances.

*Homo sapiens* crossed from Asia to North America 20,000 to 15,000 YA, by land bridge or by boat.

Humans settled in Cuba and other Caribbean islands 6,000 YA.

Settling in Indonesia and Australia 50,000 YA involved long journeys by sea.

Humans reached the islands of Polynesia around 3,000 YA.

New Zealand was perhaps the final frontier, settled just 700 YA.

Humans reached South America more than 15,000 YA.

### CAVE ART
Human fossils are rarely preserved on land. One way we trace the spread of ancient humans is by their art. These vivid animal paintings in France's Lascaux caves date back around 20,000 years. They show technical skills, creativity, and storytelling that are uniquely human.

**42,000 YA** PLEISTOCENE EPOCH

# LIFE IN THE COLD

In the Pleistocene Epoch, the world is experiencing an ice age. On the dry steppes of Eurasia, the ice has come and gone in cycles for 2.6 million years. During the periods of extreme cold, called glacials, only animals well adapted to the bitter temperatures will survive.

**1 Expanding ice**
Ice sheets grow in the north, as an extra cold period begins. A thick ice layer will soon cover the steppes, forcing animals to migrate south.

**2 Golden swoop**
A golden eagle swoops down, targeting small prey such as ground squirrels. As the ice advances, these birds of prey migrate towards ice-free areas, where more food is available.

**3 A tale of grass and ice**
Animals graze on the cool grasslands of the steppes. The active layer of soil, which thaws in summer, lies on ground that is permanently frozen, called permafrost.

**4 Woolly mammoths**
Like woolly rhinos, these mammals have fat reserves under their skin and a thick, shaggy coat that traps heat. They are about the size of an African elephant.

**5 Hungry cats**
A woolly rhino calf would make a succulent meal for a group of hungry cave lions. These large cats stalk the steppes, often on the prowl for prey.

**6 Under attack**
Steam rises from the nostrils of this woolly rhino intent on protecting its calf. Behind, an angry mother hurries over to ward off the attackers.

**7 Frozen alive**
Arctic ground squirrels emerge from underground tunnels. They hibernate to survive the coldest months, when their body temperature drops below freezing as they sleep.

# ICE AGE GIANT

There have been at least five major ice ages in Earth's history. We are living in a relatively warm period of the fifth, with ice sheets only at the poles. Woolly mammoths lived in the coldest period, and were perfectly adapted to the freezing conditions across North America and Eurasia.

Some heat escaping
Lots of heat escaping
Carbon dioxide trapping heat
Heat bouncing off Earth's surface
SUN
Trapped heat
HEAT
ATMOSPHERE
EARTH

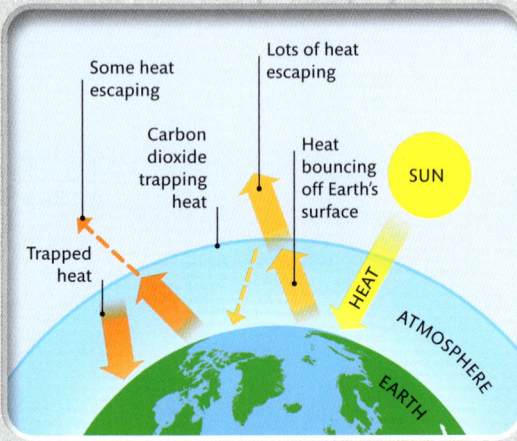

**NATURAL CLIMATE CHANGE**
Carbon dioxide traps heat in Earth's atmosphere and ice ages can happen when levels of carbon dioxide are low, the layer trapping heat is thinner, and temperatures fall. They also occur when a change in Earth's orbit tilts it away from the Sun.

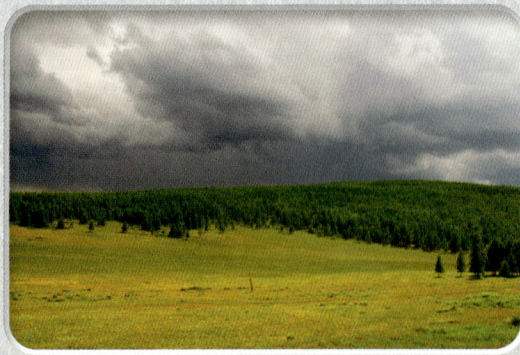

**STEPPE CHANGE**
Earth began to warm 12,000 YA. The steppe melted and formed cold, wet tundra, while conifer forests, or taiga, spread south. Without their grassland habitat, woolly mammoth numbers dwindled.

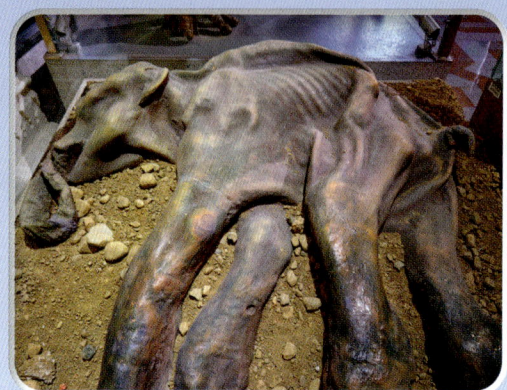

**Frozen in time**
Woolly mammoths have been found preserved in permafrost – ground that has remained frozen for years – in the northern regions of Asia and North America. The skin and tusks of this baby mammoth are remarkably intact.

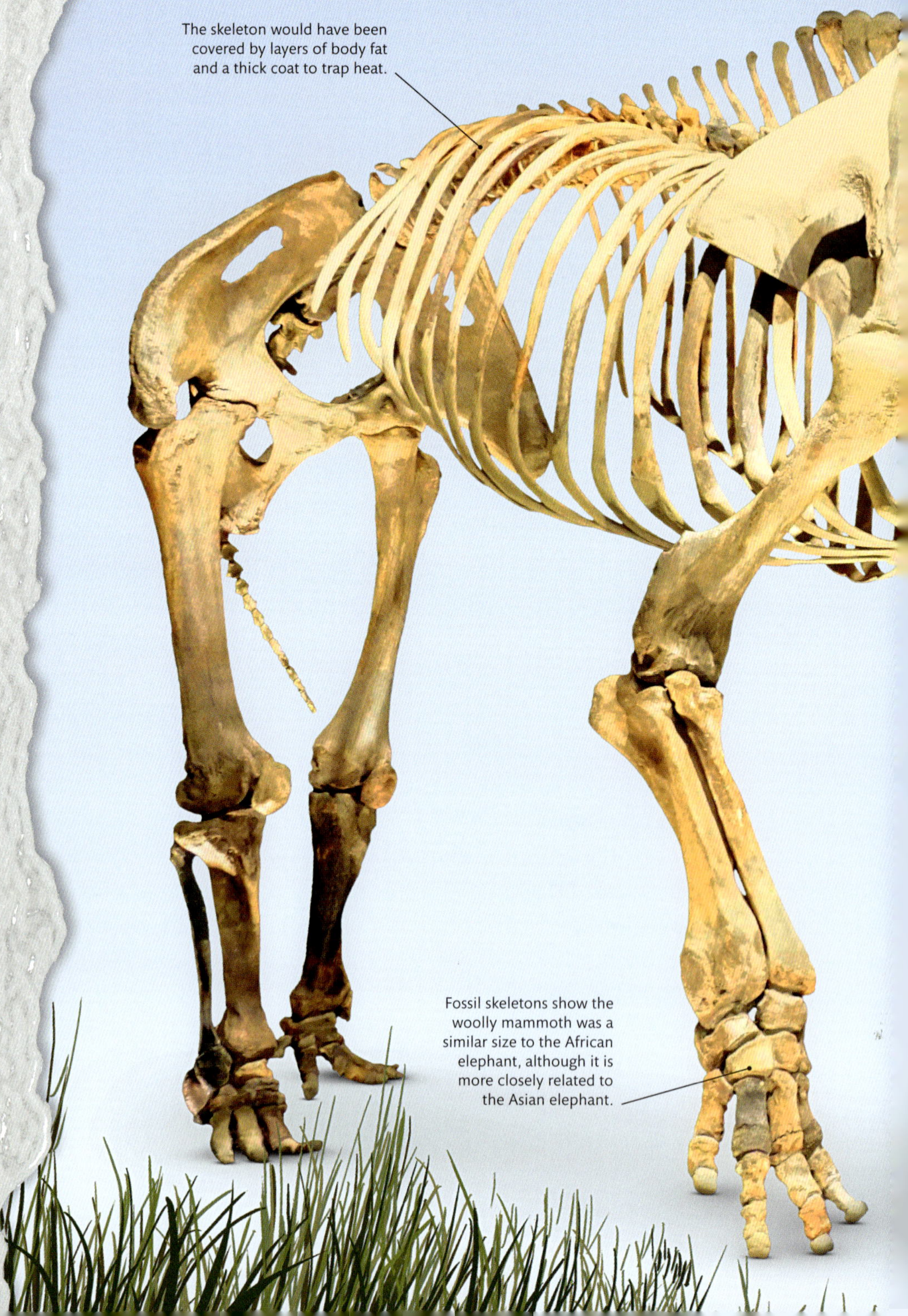

The skeleton would have been covered by layers of body fat and a thick coat to trap heat.
Fossil skeletons show the woolly mammoth was a similar size to the African elephant, although it is more closely related to the Asian elephant.

## WOOLLY MAMMOTH

Scientists know a lot about woolly mammoths from fossil skeletons and frozen specimens they have found. Humans lived at the same time as the last of them, hunting them for food, skins, and their tusks. Scientists believe it was the combined effects of global warming and hunting that led to mammoths' extinction.

**42,000–12,000 YA: Pleistocene Epoch**
As the Ice Age ended at less than one second to midnight, frozen regions thawed and sea levels rose. Many large mammals died out, including all but a handful of woolly mammoths.

The massive curved tusks were mainly used to dig under snow for food such as shrubs and grasses.

Curved tusks, on both males and females, grew up to 4 m (13 ft) long – much longer than those of modern elephants.

**Tough grinders**
Ridged teeth them to grind tough grasses. When a tooth wore down, a new one grew up behind it, pushing the old one out.

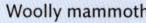
Woolly mammoth    Asian elephant

**Size comparison**

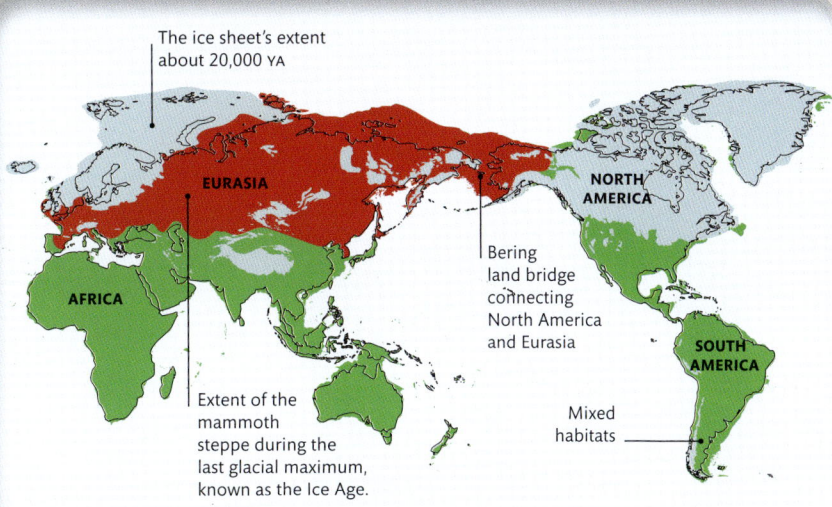

The ice sheet's extent about 20,000 YA

EURASIA

AFRICA

NORTH AMERICA

Bering land bridge connecting North America and Eurasia

SOUTH AMERICA

Mixed habitats

Extent of the mammoth steppe during the last glacial maximum, known as the Ice Age.

## MAMMOTH STEPPE

Around 20,000 YA, sea levels were much lower than today because so much water was frozen as ice. This created a land bridge that allowed mammoths to cross from Eurasia into North America. Grassland stretched from Europe to Canada – the biggest single habitat on Earth, called the mammoth steppe, where the woolly mammoths and other hardy animals grazed.

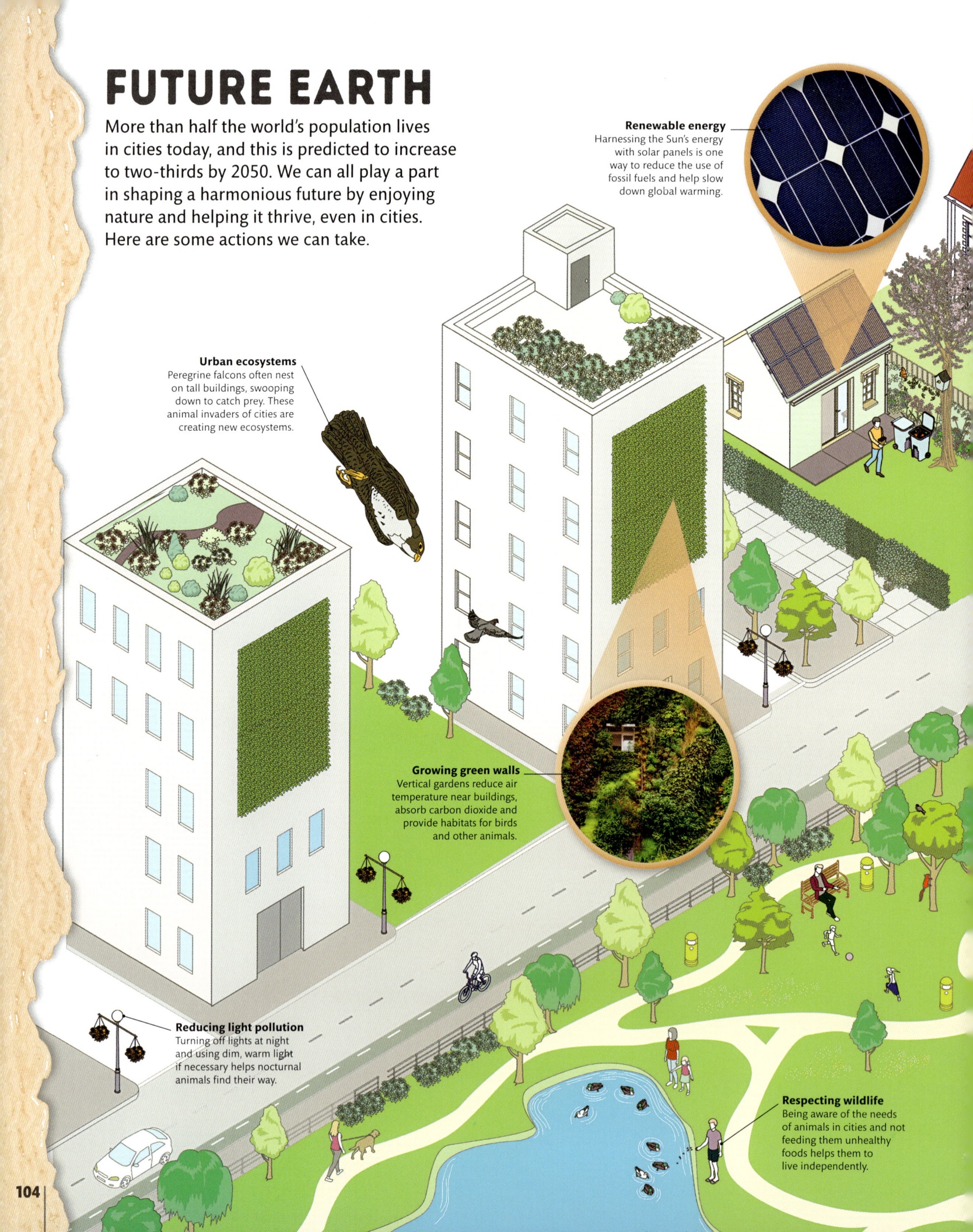

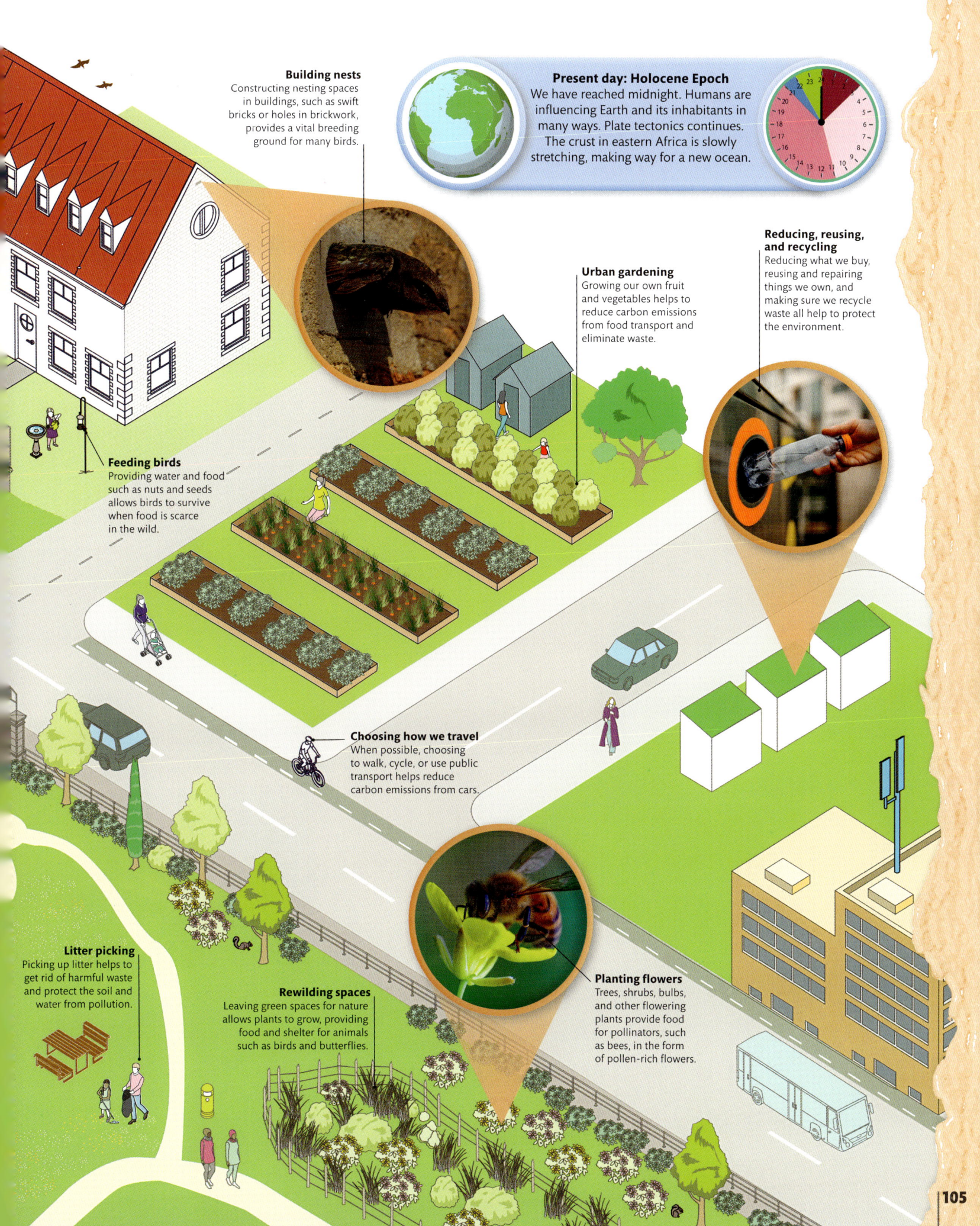

# BACK FROM THE BRINK

Human activities put many species at risk by reducing their habitats and altering the environment. The IUCN (International Union for Conservation of Nature) ranks plants and animals by extinction risk, which helps to guide conservation work to preserve endangered species. Their six levels of risk are shown in the chart below.

**THE ANTHROPOCENE**
By heating the climate and changing the environment, humans may be shaping a new geological epoch – the Anthropocene, or "Age of Humans". Future scientists might identify this epoch by the mass of discarded plastic waste – unless we act fast to remove it from land and sea.

## LEAST CONCERNED

**Peregrine falcon**
This predator is found around the globe. Once endangered in the USA, its populations recovered once the pesticide DDT was banned in the 1970s and stopped poisoning its prey.

**Eurasian red squirrel**
Grey squirrels imported from North America have driven their red cousins out of many areas. But introducing pine martens can restore the balance, as this predator catches more grey squirrels than red.

**Island night lizard**
In the 1970s, this lizard from the UK's Channel Islands was being eaten by human-bred animals such as goats and pigs. Removal of these "invasive species" has helped it recover.

## NEAR THREATENED

**Tasmanian bettong**
The bettong is under threat from new predators after red foxes and stray cats arrived in Tasmania in the last few decades. Authorities plan to remove the foxes and restore forest habitats.

**Mexican flameknee tarantula**
Illegal trade, deforestation, and loss of habitat due to farming, have depleted many Mexican tarantulas. New protection laws and careful monitoring can help preserve this colourful creature.

## VULNERABLE

**Giant anteater**
Large animals that take longer to grow and reproduce can be vulnerable to change. Giant anteaters are extinct in parts of Brazil, but programmes are afoot to reintroduce them in some areas.

**Azores bullfinch**
This bird nearly went extinct due to hunting, forest clearance, and new plants replacing their food sources. Creating protected areas and removing invasive plants are helping it to recover.

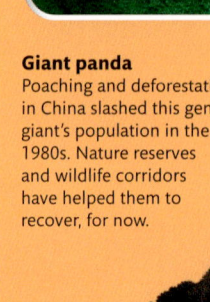

**Shortnose sturgeon**
Overfishing, pollution, and dams blocking rivers nearly drove this large North American fish extinct in the 1960s. But captive breeding and fish passages added to dams have stabilized numbers.

**Giant panda**
Poaching and deforestation in China slashed this gentle giant's population in the 1980s. Nature reserves and wildlife corridors have helped them to recover, for now.

## COMMUNITY COUNT
We can all help to preserve biodiversity. One way we can do this is to count and record species, such as the birds we see in our garden. This helps scientists create action plans.

Blue tits are common garden visitors in Europe and beyond.

## BUTTERFLY BLOOMS
By making space for wild or native flowers in our parks and gardens, we can promote insect life in cities. These flowers offer food for pollinators such as bees, butterflies, moths, and beetles. Healthy, diverse plants and insects support the entire food chain.

| ENDANGERED | CRITICALLY ENDANGERED | EXTINCT IN THE WILD |
|---|---|---|

**Zebra shark**
In 2021, only about 20 zebra sharks remained near Indonesia's Raja Ampat islands, due to overfishing and habitat loss. A rewilding project used aquarium-bred eggs to repopulate the area.

**Indigo-winged parrot**
Believed extinct for nearly a century after forests were cleared, this colourful parrot is making a comeback thanks to a "parrot corridor" of connected forest reserves in Colombia.

**Sea otter**
Fur hunting in the 18th and 19th centuries reduced sea otter numbers to about 2,000 around the North Pacific coast. International hunting bans and reintroduction efforts have boosted their numbers, but threats remain.

**Pygmy Rwandan water lily**
Before this water lily was declared extinct in the wild in 1987, scientists cultivated seeds at Kew Gardens in London, UK. Wild plants have now been found, but they need urgent protection.

**Cayman sage**
Construction work and invasive species all but wiped out Cayman Islands sage, which grows only on these islands. It was thought extinct for 40 years, but a reward poster led to the sage's rediscovery. Today, fewer than 400 plants remain.

**Christmas Island blue-tailed shinning-skink**
Last seen in the wild in 2010, this lizard was driven to near-extinction by invasive wolf snakes. Captive breeding and trial releases in protected enclosures are underway.

**Guam kingfisher**
Endemic to Guam in the Pacific Ocean, this kingfisher was wiped out in the wild by invasive brown tree snakes. Captive-bred chicks hatched on Palmyra Atoll in 2025.

**Kihansi spray toad**
Native to Tanzania, this toad declined after a dam removed the waterfall mist it relied on. Sprinklers restored the moisture, but the remaining wild toads died of disease. Captive breeding continues.

# TIMELINE OF EARTH

Over its 4.5-billion-year history, Earth has experienced dramatic transformations, from a molten sphere to a frozen globe, a water world to an ever-reshuffling jigsaw of continents. As energy deep within our planet keeps shifting and remaking the Earth's crust, it has formed a series of worlds very different from the one we know today. These images show Earth from the same angle at intervals through its lifetime.

**Molten Earth, 4.5 BYA**
When Earth first formed it was a hot ball of molten rock called magma. Its surface was constantly bombarded by meteorites.

**500 MYA**
In the southern hemisphere were several continents flooded by shallow seas. These saw an explosion of new life forms.

**380 MYA**
The first forests and animals had conquered the land. Shallow coastal seas, teeming with life, began to shrink as continents slowly merged.

**300 MYA**
Continents assembled in a single, massive landmass or supercontinent named Pangaea, surrounded by a vast ocean called Panthalassa.

**80 MYA**
Vast inland seas spilled into continents. Dinosaurs thrived on land, flowering plants and pollinators flourished, and birds and mammals diversified.

**66 MYA**
As continents approached their modern positions, Earth was warm and humid. A huge asteroid crashed into Earth and all dinosaurs except birds died out.

**40 MYA**
High levels of carbon dioxide in the air meant Earth was warmer than today, and free of polar ice sheets. Mammals diversified and thrived.

**Cooling Earth, 3.8 BYA**
Earth cooled enough for the first solid rocks to form a crust on its surface and water to condense into oceans.

**Snowball Earth, 700 MYA**
Ice engulfed most of the globe, though some ice-free or slushy areas remained. During thawing periods, algae flourished in the oceans.

**600 MYA**
The ice melted, releasing nutrients into the oceans, where the first complex, multicellular organisms formed. Land was clustered around the South Pole.

**250 MYA**
Pangaea's centre, far from the sea, was dry and barren. The Great Dying *(see pages 48–49)* had wiped out 90 per cent of all species on Earth.

**180 MYA**
Pangaea started to break apart into two landmasses, Laurasia in the north and Gondwana in the south. Marine reptiles filled the seas.

**120 MYA**
By now, South America had started to separate from Africa, while India was drifting north towards Asia. Dinosaurs ruled the land.

**21,000 YA**
The latest ice age reached its peak. Soon after, gradual warming began, allowing humans to enter North America.

*Present day*

# GLOSSARY

Gomphothere

**AMMONITE**
An extinct sea creature with a spiral shell, related to modern-day squid and octopus.

**APOLLO MISSIONS**
A series of crewed space missions to observe and explore the Moon in the 1960s and 1970s.

**BILATERAL SYMMETRY**
This means that one side of an animal or plant is a mirror image of the other, either side of a centre line. Mammals, birds, reptiles, and fish all have bilateral symmetry between left and right sides.

**BROW RIDGE**
Horizontal bone above the eye, which sticks out in some species of ancient human.

**CARCASS**
The dead body of an animal.

**CARNIVORE**
An animal that mostly eats other animals.

**CAST**
A fossil formed when minerals replace the dead body of an animal after it decomposes. *See also mould.*

**CONVERGENT EVOLUTION**
A case where two different species independently develop the same adaptation to their environment. For example, ice age rhinos and mammoths both developed warm coats.

**CORE**
Earth's centre, made up of two parts: a solid metallic inner core and a liquid metallic outer core.

**CRUST**
The thin, cool, solid outer layer of Earth on which all animals and plants live.

**CYANOBACTERIA**
Tiny single-celled organisms that can make food using the energy of sunlight by photosynthesis, as most plants do today.

**FAULT**
A crack in the Earth's crust – these form the boundaries between tectonic plates.

**FISHAPOD**
An animal partway between water-dwelling fish with fins and four-legged land animals (called tetrapods), such as *Tiktaalik*.

**GONDWANA**
A huge landmass that formed near the South Pole more than 600 MYA. It later merged into the supercontinent Pangaea, then separated again and split to form Africa, South America, India, Antarctica, and Australia.

**HERBIVORE**
An animal that mostly eats plants and fungi.

**LAURASIA**
A huge landmass that formed around 200 MYA during the break-up of Pangaea. It included modern-day Asia, Europe, and North America.

**LOBE-FINNED FISH**
Fleshy-finned fish, such as coelacanths and the ancestors of tetrapods that evolved to walk on land.

**MANGROVE**
Trees that grow along muddy seashores and tolerate the salt of seawater.

**MANTLE**
Thick layer of putty-like, part-molten rock that makes up most of Earth's interior.

**MASTODON**
A large extinct mammal similar to a mammoth or a modern-day elephant.

**MEGAFAUNA EXTINCTION EVENT**
Period from around 50,000 to 5,000 YA, when 80 per cent of large mammal species went extinct, likely due to human hunters.

**METAMORPHIC ROCK**
Rock that has been fundamentally changed by extreme heat or pressure.

**MOLTEN**
Changed from a solid state to a more liquid state by heat or pressure.

**MOULD**
A hollow impression left in rock by a dead animal before it rots away. *See also cast.*

**NOTOUNGULATE**
A large and varied family of South American mammals that lived from around 60 MYA until 11,000 YA.

**NUCLEUS**
The command centre of a living cell, containing instructions for how it forms and behaves.

**OPOSSUM**
Marsupial found in North, Central, or South America, and related to Australian marsupials such as kangaroos and possums.

**PALAEONTOLOGIST**
A scientist who studies fossilized animals and plants.

**PANGAEA**
A supercontinent that contained most of Earth's land from around 320 MYA to 180 MYA.

**PLACODERM FISH**
An extinct group of prehistoric fish with an armour-plated head and chest.

**RADIAL SYMMETRY**
Refers to the circular or star-like body shape of an animal, such as a starfish, composed of matching parts around a central point.

Ancient magnolia flower

**RODINIA**
A supercontinent containing most of Earth's land, which formed 1.2 BYA and broke up around 750 MYA.

**SAVANNAH**
Open, dry grassland with scattered trees and bushes, typically in Africa.

**SEDIMENTARY ROCK**
Rock formed by layers of sediment (rock fragments) laid down and compressed by further layers of sediment over millions of years.

**SPORES**
Single cells released into the air by organisms such as ferns and fungi in order to reproduce.

**SUBDUCTION**
Process by which a denser oceanic plate is forced under a lighter continental plate as they collide.

**SUPERCONTINENT**
A huge landmass comprising two or more of today's continents. *See also Pangaea and Rodinia.*

**SYMBIOTIC**
Any relationship between different kinds of interacting organisms. Some of these benefit all organisms involved, others just one of them.

**TECTONIC PLATES**
Large pieces of Earth's crust that move relative to each other.

**TETRAPOD**
An animal with four limbs and a backbone, such as all reptiles, mammals, and birds.

**UNGULATE**
A mammal with hooves, usually a plant-eater.

*Tiktaalik*

Camelid

# INDEX

## A
*Aglaophyton* 36
algae 19, 21, 24-25
*Allosaurus* 68
amber 64
ammonites 49, 54, 56-57
ammonoids 45
amphibians 46, 51, 107
Andes Mountains 80, 89
angiosperms 63
*Ankylosaurus* 66
*Anomalocaris* 33, 34-35
Antarctica 84-87
Anthropocene Epoch 106
*Anzu wyliei* 66
Archaean Eon 16-21
*Archaeopteryx* 61
*Archaeorhynchus* 59
arthropods 27, 33, 34-35, 36, 39
    see also insects
asteroids 15, 51, 70-73
*Asteroxylon* 36
Atlantic Ocean 82, 92, 94
atmosphere 15, 19, 23, 102
*Australopithecus africanus* 98
*Avicennia* 80

## B
Baltica 43
bears 90
beetles 63, 64-65
belemnites 54
birds 61, 73, 101, 106-107
    penguins 80, 84-87
brachiopods 45, 49
bristle worms 33

## C
*Cambaytherium* 76
Cambrian Period 32-35
camelids 90
Carboniferous Period 44-47
caviomorphs 80
*Cheirolepis* 41
climate change 102
*Cloudina* 30
club mosses 36, 47
*Coahuilaceratops* 71
coal 46
coelacanths 41
*Confuciusornis* 59
continental drift 16, 23, 76, 108-109
corals 45
Cretaceous Period 58-59, 60, 62-67, 69, 82
mass extinction 51, 70-73
crinoids 45, 49
crust 15, 16-17, 78-79
cyanobacteria 12-13, 19, 21
*Cyclomedusa* 30

## D
deserts 94
Devonian Period 36-43, 50
*Diacodexis* 76
*Dickinsonia* 28
*Dilong* 58
dinosaurs 6, 51, 52-53, 58-60, 66-71
*Diplodocus* 68

## E
eagles 101
earthquakes 78, 92
ecosystems 82, 104
Ediacaran Period 28-31
*Edmontosaurus* 52-53, 66
Eocene Epoch 76-87
*Eomorphippus* 89
*Eoraptor* 68
*Eotriceratops* 52-53
*Eovisaccia* 89
*Ernietta* 31
erosion 92
eukaryotes 20
extinction 48-51, 70-73, 106-107
extraterrestrial life 21

## F
ferns 39, 47, 63, 71
fish 51, 54, 85, 106
    Palaeozoic Era 33, 38, 39, 40-41
flooding 92-95
flowering plants 62-63, 105
forests 38-39, 47, 80-83, 86
fossils 7, 30, 42-43, 57
    ammonites 49, 54, 56-57
    stromatolites 12-13, 19, 21
    trilobites 26-27, 34, 49
fungi 36
*Funisia* 28

## G
gastropods 45
geological dating 7
ginkgo trees 63
glaciers 24, 25, 85
*Glikmanius* 45
*Glyptodon* 91
gomphotheres 90
Gondwana 16, 85, 87
grasslands 91, 96, 102, 103
gymnosperms 63

## H
Hadean Eon 8-11, 14-15
hadrosaurs 71
*Hallucigenia* 33
*Helicolocellus* 31
Himalayan Mountains 76, 77-78
holdfasts 28
Holocene Period 51, 105
*Homo erectus* 96, 98
*Homo sapiens* 98-99
*Horneophyton* 36
horsetails 47
hot springs 20, 36
humans 6, 51, 87, 96-97, 98-99, 106
*Hybodus* 54
hydrothermal vents 21

## I
ice ages 23, 24, 100-101, 102
ichthyosaurs 54
*Iguanodon* 69
*Inkayacu* 80
*Inostrancevia* 49
insects 39, 46, 47, 63, 64-65
Isthmus of Panama 90

## J
Jurassic Period 54-55, 57, 61, 69

## K
*Kimberella* 28

## L
*Labocania* 71
Laurasia 16, 43
Laurentia 43
lava 15, 49
*Leedsichthys* 54
lichens 36
lignite 46
*Liopleurodon* 54
lizards 76, 106
*Llanocetus* 85
*Longipteryx* 59

## M
magnolias 62-65, 71
*Maiasaura* 69
mammals 51, 69, 73, 106-107
    Cenozoic Era 76, 80, 86, 88-91
    mammoths, woolly 74-75, 101, 102-103
marine animals 28-35, 44-45, 49, 94, 106-107
    Jurassic Period 54-57
    see also fish; penguins
*Marrella* 33
marsupials 89, 91
mass extinction 48-51, 70-73
mayflies 63
Mediterranean Sea 92-95
Mesozoic Era 69
meteorites 9, 15, 20
millipedes 38, 47
Miocene Epoch 76-79, 91
molluscs 45, 54, 56, 94
monkeys 80, 82
Moon, the 10-11, 15
mountains 76-79
multicellular life 6, 20, 23, 24, 30-31

## N
nautiluses 57
North America 90
notoungulates 89

## O
oceans 10, 16-17, 19, 23, 78
    Zanclean Megaflood 92-94
    see also marine animals
Oligocene Epoch 84-85, 88-89
*Opabinia* 33
opossums 89
Ordovician Period 38, 50
oviraptors 66

## P
*Palaeeudyptes* 85, 86
*Palaeocharinus* 36
Palaeogene Period 82, 83, 91
Pangaea 16, 49, 50, 57, 64
Panthalassa 50
*Paranthropus boisei* 98
*Pareiasaurus* 49
peat 46
*Pelagornithids* 85
penguins 80, 84-87
permafrost 101, 102
Permian Period 48-51
*Perupithecus* 80
photosynthesis 19, 21
*Pikaia* 33
plants 6, 36-39, 46-47, 62-65, 82-83
plate tectonics 16
Pleistocene Epoch 89, 96-103
plesiosaurs 54
Pliocene Epoch 92-95
pollinators 63-65, 107
prokaryotes 6, 20
Proterozoic Eon 18-19, 22-25
*Prototaxites* 36

## Q
*Quetzalcoatlus* 71

## R
rainforests 82-83
reptiles 49, 73, 80, 106
*Rhynia* 36
*Rhyniella* 36
rock cycle 7
Rodinia 23, 25, 30

## S
*Sahelanthropus tchadensis* 98
*Sciadophyton* 36
sea lilies 45
seasons 11
seaweeds 24
sharks 45, 54, 85, 107
single-cell life 6, 20, 24
*Sinosauropteryx* 59
sloths 89, 91
South America 89, 90-91
*Spriggina* 28, 30
steppes 102, 103
*Stethacanthus* 45
stromatolites 12-13, 19, 21
*Struthiomimus* 69
subduction 17, 89
swamps 45, 46-47

## T
tapirs 90
tetrapods 41, 42
Theia 10-11
theropods 59, 60
*Thescelosaurus* 66
*Thylacosmilus* 91
tides 10
*Tiktaalik* 41
timeline of Earth 108-109
*Toxodon* 89, 91
trees 38-39, 47, 59
    Cenozoic Era 80-83, 85, 86
    see also forests
Triassic Period 51, 54, 69
*Tribrachidium* 28, 30
*Triceratops* 66
trilobites 26-27, 34, 49
tsunamis 71, 73
*Tyrannosaurus rex* 60, 66

## V
vascular plants 36, 38
*Vauxia* 33
*Velociraptor* 60
volcanoes 15, 23, 78, 89, 90
    and extinction events 49, 50, 72

## W
wasps 65
waterfalls 95
whales 85
*Wiwaxia* 33
woolly mammoths 74-75, 101, 102-103
woolly rhinos 101

## Y
*Yixianosaurus* 59
*Yutyrannus* 59

## Z
Zanclean Megaflood 92, 94

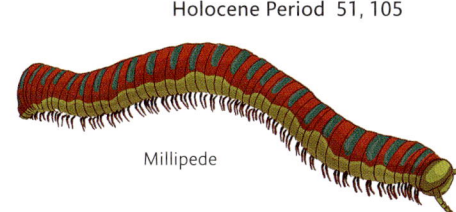
Millipede

Sea lilies
*Stethacanthus* shark

# ACKNOWLEDGMENTS

DK would like to thank: John Hort for the idea; Beth Johnston, Simon Mumford, and Kit Lane for additional design; Binta Jallow and Georgina Palffy for additional editing; Catherine Saunders for proofreading; Elizabeth Wise for the index; Sumedha Chopra for picture research; Mik Gates for visualization; and Phil Gamble for additional illustration.

The publisher would like to thank the following for their kind permission to reproduce their photographs:
(Key: a-above; b-below/bottom; c-centre; f-far; l-left; r-right; t-top)

**6 Getty Images / iStock:** photohampster (bl). **7 Dorling Kindersley:** Colin Keates / Natural History Museum, London (crb). **8 Getty Images:** Stocktrek Images (clb). **9 Dreamstime.com:** Kriscole (cr). **Shutterstock.com:** abriendomundo (cra). **10-11 Shutterstock.com:** Jacques Dayan. **12-13 Alamy Stock Photo:** Jiri Lochman / Nature Picture Library. **14-15 Alamy Stock Photo:** Science Photo Library / Mark Garlick. **Shutterstock.com:** Thijs Peters (b). **17 Getty Images:** Ralph Lee Hopkins / Design Pics Editorial / Universal Images (tc). **20 Adobe Stock:** VectorMine (t). **Alamy Stock Photo:** Connect Images / Yevgen Timashov. **21 Alamy Stock Photo:** Science Photo Library / Christoph Burgstedt (r). **Dreamstime.com:** Galih Wisnu (l). **22-23 Science Photo Library:** Chris Butler. **24 Getty Images / iStock:** Robert_Ford (bl). **25 Science Photo Library:** Chris Butler (bc). **26-27 Alamy Stock Photo:** Roland Bouvier. **30 Alamy Stock Photo:** Pacific Imagica (tc). **Dorling Kindersley:** Simon Mumford / Colorado Plateau Geosystems Inc. (bl). **34 Science Photo Library:** Sinclair Stammers (bl). **35 Dorling Kindersley:** Simon Mumford / Colorado Plateau Systems Inc. (bc). **38 Dreamstime.com:** Witold Krasowski (bl). **Getty Images / iStock:** slowmotiongli (clb). **39 Dorling Kindersley:** Simon Mumford / Colorado Plateau Systems Inc. (tl). **42 Science Photo Library:** John Sibbick (cla). **43 Alamy Stock Photo:** Corbin17 (cr); Jim West (cra). **Dorling Kindersley:** Simon Mumford / Colorado Plateau Systems Inc. (bl). **47 Dorling Kindersley:** Simon Mumford / Colorado Plateau Systems Inc. (bl). **Science Photo Library:** Philippe Psaila (cra). **50 Dorling Kindersley:** Simon Mumford / Colorado Plateau Systems Inc. (c). **Getty Images / iStock:** Beboy_ltd (tc). **Science Photo Library:** Gwen Shockey (br). **Shutterstock.com:** Aunt Spray (bc). **51 Dreamstime.com:** William Roberts (cl). **Getty Images / iStock:** Warpaintcobra (cra). **52-53 Science Photo Library:** Julius T Csotonyi. **57 Alamy Stock Photo:** NorthScape (tr). **Dorling Kindersley:** Simon Mumford / Colorado Plateau Geosystems Inc. (tl). **Dreamstime.com:** Antonio Ribeiro (cr). **Shutterstock.com:** wildestanimal (br). **61 Dorling Kindersley:** Colin Keates / Natural History Museum, London (bl); Simon Mumford / Colorado Plateau Systems Inc. (tl). **Getty Images / iStock:** nadtytok (cb). **Science Photo Library:** Steve Gschmeissner (bc). **69 Alamy Stock Photo:** Nicolas Fernandez (tc). **Dorling Kindersley:** Simon Mumford / Colorado Plateau Systems Inc. (cb). **72 Science Photo Library:** David A. Kring (clb). **73 Dorling Kindersley:** Simon Mumford / Colorado Plateau Geosystems Inc. (bl). **Dreamstime.com:** Elantsev (crb). **Science Photo Library:** Prof. Walter Alvarez (tc). **Shutterstock.com:** Wim Hoek (crb/tinamou). **74-75 Alamy Stock Photo:** Science Picture Co. **79 Dorling Kindersley:** Simon Mumford / Colorado Plateau Systems Inc. (bc). **82 Getty Images / iStock:** Sorranop (cla). **86 Alamy Stock Photo:** Brian Anderson (cla). **87 Alamy Stock Photo:** All Canada Photos / Wayne Lynch (tr); NG Images (cr). **Dorling Kindersley:** Simon Mumford / Colorado Plateau Systems Inc. (tl). **Dreamstime.com:** Inaras (br); Sergey Korotkov (bc). **Getty Images / iStock:** kotomiti (l). **94 Alamy Stock Photo:** Mint Photography (cl). **Dorling Kindersley:** Simon Mumford / Colorado Plateau Systems Inc. (bc). Artur Tomaszek (clb). **99 Alamy Stock Photo:** CPA Media Pte Ltd / Pictures From History (bl). **102 Alamy Stock Photo:** Worawan Simaroj (clb); James Talalay (tc). **102-103 Alamy Stock Photo:** Peter van Evert. **103 Dreamstime.com:** Planetfelicity (cr). **Getty Images:** Corbis Documentary / Walter Geiersperger (clb). **104 Getty Images / iStock:** MoreISO (tr); pixelprof (cb). **105 Alamy Stock Photo:** Simon Stirrup (cla). **Dorling Kindersley:** Simon Mumford / Colorado Plateau Systems Inc. (tc). **Getty Images / iStock:** apodiam (cb); urbazon / E+ (cra). **106 123RF.com:** Eric Isselee / isselee (ca). **Alamy Stock Photo:** Buiten-Beeld / Daniele Occhiato (cr); imageBROKER / Andrey Nekrasov (tc); Nature Picture Library / Chris Mattison (bl); Heinz Erich Zappel (crb). **Dreamstime.com:** Brian Kushner / Bkushner (cl); Wirestock (c); Isselee (clb). **Fotolia:** Eric Isselee (br). **Getty Images:** DikkyOesin (bc). **107 Alamy Stock Photo:** John Bentley (tc); Rieger Bertrand / Hemis.fr (cl); Tim Gainey (c). **Dreamstime.com:** Dleindec (br); Kuritafsheen (cr); Vaclav Sebek (clb); Michaelfitzsimmons (crb); Hotshotsworldwide (bl). **Getty Images:** Akinori Okade / 500px (bc). **Getty Images / iStock:** CathyDoi (tl)